Grundwortschatz Englisch · Vocabulary Exercises

Grundlage für das vorliegende Übungsbuch ist:

Grund- und Aufbauwortschatz Englisch

Bearbeitet von Erich Weis
276 Seiten, Klettbuch 51951

Dieser Band enthält mit ihren deutschen Bedeutungen 4500 englische Wörter – ausgewählt nach ihrem Häufigkeitswert, dem die internationalen Forschungen auf dem Gebiet der Worthäufigkeit zugrunde liegen. Sie sind aufgeteilt in

2000 Wörter Grundwortschatz
(in alphabetischer Ordnung)

2500 Wörter Aufbauwortschatz
(nach Sachgruppen geordnet).

Darüber hinaus werden Sätze und idiomatische Redewendungen gebracht, die – nach dem Prinzip der Worthäufigkeit zusammengestellt – eine wertvolle Bereicherung der Ausdrucksfähigkeit bilden.
Mit Hilfe des alphabetischen Registers zum Aufbauwortschatz – für die Fremdsprache und das Deutsche – läßt sich schnell feststellen, ob ein bestimmtes Wort im Aufbauwortschatz vorhanden ist, in welcher Sachgruppe es sich befindet und, bei Wörtern aus den Sätzen und Redewendungen, in welchem Kontext es am häufigsten gebraucht wird.

Grundwortschatz Englisch

Vocabulary Exercises

by Lawrence G. Morgan and Roy E. Ogren

Ernst Klett Verlag für Wissen und Bildung

Contents

Foreword 5
A for Adventure 7
B for Beginning 16
C for Compare 25
D for Discover 35
E for Experience 43
F for Familiar 50
G for Grow 58
H for Happen 64
I for Idea (with J and K) 71
L for Love 78
M for Mail 87
N for Necessary 96
O for Opinion 100
P for Practical (with Q) 106
R for Radio 119
S for Smile 128
T for Touch 144
U and V for Unusual View 155
WXY and Z 160

1. Auflage 1 15 14 13 12 | 1993 92 91 90

Alle Drucke dieser Auflage können im Unterricht nebeneinander benutzt werden, sie sind untereinander unverändert. Die letzte Zahl bezeichnet das Jahr dieses Druckes.

Druck: Gutmann + Co., Heilbronn. Printed in Germany.
ISBN 3-12-519520-9

Foreword

If you want to learn to improve your spoken and written English, this book will be of great value to you. It offers exercises and tests based on the 2,000 most frequently used words in the English language. You will find these words in the book *Grund- und Aufbauwortschatz Englisch* by Professor Erich Weis.

This, however, is only the beginning. Your success will depend on the effort you put into your work and the way you work. Every good sportsman must train regularly in order to achieve good results. In the same way, every student of a language needs regular practice and revision.

Try to observe these simple rules:

1. Work regularly. If you practise for 20 minutes every day, you will learn twice as much as if you work for 2 hours once a week.
2. Always revise what you have learnt before you go on to something new. Each chapter of this book deals with words which begin with the same letter. Before you start the exercises in a chapter, first make sure you know all the words in the *Grundwortschatz Englisch* which begin with that letter.
3. Practise difficult words again and again. Even if you are a quick learner, there will always be some words which are difficult for you to remember. Write these down in a note-book and revise them frequently.
4. Be honest with yourself. Do all the exercises in a chapter before you look at the answer key, and then count up your mistakes. If you have made too many mistakes, the best thing to do is to look through the words in the *Grundwortschatz* once more and then repeat the whole chapter.

If you observe these simple "training rules", you will achieve your aim quickly and without too much trouble. Before long you will be able to say: "Now I understand English much better than I did before, and soon I will be able to speak it fluently!"

For the Teacher

With the aid of this book the student can acquire an active and passive command of the basic English Vocabulary. The exercises in each chapter test the ability of the student to: a) recognize the correct word from a number of alternatives (Exercise group I—VI); and b) provide and insert the correct word in a clear context (Exercise group VII—X).

Group a) Word Recognition:

I—III	Multiple choice. The student must select the correct antonym (I), synonym (II), or complementary phrase (III) from a list of three alternatives.
IV	Recognition of true or false statements and definitions.
V	Recognition of nouns which are related according to their sense.
VI	Recognition of words which belong together to form certain structures.

Group b) Word Insertion:

VII—IX	Exercises in which the correct noun (VII), verb (VIII), or adjective/adverb/preposition (IX) must be inserted in a clear context.
X	Exercises which test idiomatic use of the language at a more difficult level. The word to be inserted may begin with any letter of the alphabet and may be any part of speech. It always, however, forms part of a phrase or expression which is listed in the respective chapter.

A for Adventure

You are *about to* begin a great *adventure! As soon as* you know English well, you will have many *advantages at home and abroad. Among other things,* you are certain to make new *acquaintances. Aim high! Above all,* don't be *afraid* of hard work! *Attempt* to find *answers* for each problem. You will *acquire* new words every day. *Go ahead!*

I. What's the opposite?

1. What's the *answer* to this
   a) quality?
   b) question?
   c) quarter?

2. *Dead* people are not
   a) alive.
   b) asleep.
   c) available.

3. Single people live *alone;* married people live
   a) apart.
   b) separately.
   c) together.

4. The future is *ahead of* us. The past is
   a) behind us.
   b) beside us.
   c) before us.

5. If someone *attacks* me, I must
   a) introduce myself.
   b) enjoy myself.
   c) defend myself.

6. I brush my teeth *after* I eat, not
   a) during.
   b) until.
   c) before.

7. The train from New York City *arrives* at six and
   a) enters at eight.
   b) leaves at seven.
   c) signals at seven.

8. Ten students were *absent* from school. The rest were
   a) missing.
   b) present.
   c) early.

9. Are you *for* or
   a) above social change?
   b) apart from social change?
   c) against social change?

10. Some people *approved of* the new tax, but most
    a) objected to it.
    b) enjoyed it.
    c) welcomed it.

II. Which word or phrase has almost the same meaning?

1. The doctor came *right away.*
   a) later on
   b) immediately
   c) afterwards

2. *Ancient* buildings are
   a) very old.
   b) up-to-date.
   c) modern.

3. *Armed* soldiers
   a) have two arms.
   b) carry weapons.
   c) never fight.

4. The two brothers look *alike.*
   a) the same
   b) strange
   c) different

5. *At last* spring is here!
   a) before long
   b) finally
   c) at one time

6. How much have you *actually* got?
   a) in fact
   b) probably
   c) always

7. My *aunt* is my
   a) mother's or father's brother.
   b) mother's or father's sister.
   c) mother's or father's father.

8. *Time and again* you make the same mistake!
   a) hardly ever
   b) over and over again
   c) sometimes

9. *All day long* people came to the fair.
   a) for many days
   b) in the morning
   c) throughout the day

10. Cats *are afraid of* dogs.
    a) admire
    b) fear
    c) love

11. Twenty members *attended* the meeting.
    a) organized
    b) paid attention to
    c) came to

12. This rule does not *apply to* you.
    a) concern
    b) confuse
    c) convince

13. Please *ask for* two copies!
    a) remove
    b) request
    c) require

14. People travelling abroad always have to *get accustomed to* new food.
    a) get used to
    b) get away from
    c) get rid of

15. Smoking is not *allowed* here.
    a) required
    b) permitted
    c) forbidden

16. His bad behaviour made me *angry*.
    a) cross
    b) happy
    c) cheerful

17. Please *answer* this letter right away!
    a) refuse
    b) reply to
    c) resist

18. I *accidentally* cut my finger!
    a) on purpose
    b) by mistake
    c) nearly

19. *On account of* the strike, no buses were running.
    a) before
    b) besides
    c) because of

Does the next exercise *appear* difficult? It's true — it's *not at all* easy! *As* you *approach* each exercise, remember that every mistake you make *acquaints* you *with* a new word or idea. Don't be *ashamed of* not knowing an *answer!*

III. Which choice makes sense?

1. The horses are ready. The race is
   a) almost over!
   b) about to start!
   c) already run!

2. I can't afford to buy a new car.
   a) It's too expensive.
   b) I have too much money.
   c) I love to drive.

3. Must we always argue?
   a) Can't we ever complain?
   b) Can't we ever agree?
   c) Can't we ever worry?

4. I can't agree to that.
   a) It's a wonderful idea.
   b) I don't approve of it.
   c) I'm in favour of it.

5. Put that aside.
   a) I want to sit down there.
   b) It can wait until tomorrow.
   c) I'm a stranger here.

6. I don't know anything about it.
   a) I was out of town at the time.
   b) I'm in charge here.
   c) I saw it happen.

7. That's my affair.
   a) It belongs to me.
   b) I don't want to hear about it.
   c) It's none of your business.

8. What's the use anyhow?
   a) No sooner said than done.
   b) I'll never make it.
   c) Make yourself at home.

9. I attach considerable importance to what you've said, and
   a) it doesn't matter in the least.
   b) I'll give it serious consideration.
   c) I don't believe a word of it.

IV. Is it true or false?

	T	F
1. Active men are lazy.	☐	☐
2. An apple is an animal.	☐	☐
3. All people look alike.	☐	☐
4. Appearances are often deceiving.	☐	☐
5. After day comes night.	☐	☐
6. Children amuse themselves by playing.	☐	☐
7. Doctors attend to their patients.	☐	☐
8. Works of art are always small.	☐	☐
9. Criminals avoid the police.	☐	☐
10. Accidents are caused purposely.	☐	☐
11. A person often admires his best friend.	☐	☐
12. Good friends always take advantage of one another.	☐	☐

Don't *fall asleep* now! *Pay attention to* each new word. Your progress will *astonish* you!

V. Find the nouns which go together.

1. article
2. arm
3. aunt
4. amount
5. advantage
6. application
7. apple
8. animal
9. ashes
10. army
11. admission
12. autumn
13. acquaintance
14. association

a) ticket, b) sum, c) job, d) club, e) newspaper, f) friend, g) hand, h) fire, i) season, j) uncle, k) fruit, l) dog, m) disadvantage, n) soldier

VI. Find the words which go together.

1. to put ..... 3. to fall ..... 5. to let .....
2. to attend ..... 4. to pay ..... 6. to ask .....

a) asleep, b) attention, c) a question, d) alone, e) aside, f) a meeting

VII. Put in the right noun.

1. We moved last week. Our new ..... is 17, Oak Street.
2. During World War II, thousands of soldiers were killed in .....
3. Without attracting ....., the thief entered the house.
4. Newspaper ..... report world and local events.
5. Lions, bears, horses, sheep and birds are all .....
6. After my trip abroad, I had almost no money left in my bank .....
7. People who climb mountains and explore space lead lives which are full of .....
8. Last week my uncle was seriously injured in a car .....
9. The theatre was quiet as the curtain rose for the third ..... of the play.
10. "Let's open the windows and let in some fresh .....!"
11. In spite of serious political differences, the two nations were able to work out a trade .....
12. ..... to the park was free, but we had to pay to go into the house.
13. My ..... was successful, and I got the job.
14. .....is a state of mind which develops from extreme worry.
15. "I can't give you an ..... with Doctor Smith before next Tuesday."
16. "What's the ..... of your youngest son?"
17. A successful merchant knows that good ..... will help him to sell more.
18. ..... are deceiving. In other words, things aren't always what they seem to be.
19. "I'll act on your ..... You've always been right in the past."
20. We had to make a lot of ..... for the party, such as ordering the food and drink and sending out invitations.
21. In a large city you will see people carrying out all kinds of ..... — buying and selling things, driving cars, working in offices, and children playing in the parks.
22. Good ..... — whether music, painting or writing — helps a person to see or experience something in a new way.

You are *already acquainted with* many new words. Each exercise increases your *ability* to *apply* these words. Are you *anxious* to succeed? Then *at all costs* complete these sentences *right away*!

VIII. Put in the right verb.

1. How fast can you ..... up this list of numbers?
2. Good opportunities often ..... when you can't take advantage of them.
3. When I heard your side of the story, I had to ..... that I was wrong.
4. The police ..... the young man for attempted murder.
5. I have always ..... my best friend for his patience.
6. The police asked the man to ..... for his actions over the last 24 hours.
7. When the lion was near enough, the man raised his gun, ... and fired.
8. I would like to ..... your invitation to supper, but I already have other plans.
9. The patient ..... on his doctor's advice and stayed in bed for a week.
10. Before the judge, the criminals refused to ..... that they were guilty.
11. The hotel bill ..... to £8.
12. It was so cold outside that I ..... the postman in for a cup of coffee.
13. No one in the bank was able to ..... for the missing money.
14. Although his friends ..... him against it, Richard left school and got a job.
15. When the firm's present representative retires, the manager will have to ..... a new one.
16. Can you ..... a meeting for me with the manager early next week?
17. As the train ..... the station, the passengers prepared to get off.
18. When you ..... for a job, you must first fill out an application form.
19. On his first day of school, I ..... my young brother to his class, because he was afraid to go alone.
20. When you consider how busy he is, it ..... me that he finds so much time to spend with his family.

IX. Put in the right adjective, adverb, or preposition.

1. Young children are often ..... of the dark.
2. The beginnings of the modern world can be traced back to ..... civilizations.
3. The two men rowed ..... the Atlantic Ocean from America to Ireland.
4. After three months abroad, I was quite ..... to see my family again.

5. ..... the shore you can see a variety of sea life, rocks of all colours and many beautiful small shells.
6. That's the ..... truth, whether you believe it or not.
7. "We haven't any shoes in your size in stock, but they should be ..... next week."
8. Towards the end of the race, no one could tell which horse was .....
9. Many groups in which he is ..... seek social reform.
10. By midnight I was so tired that I couldn't stay ..... a minute longer!
11. Jim leaned his bicycle ..... the wall.
12. After we had argued, my wife and I were so ..... with one another that we didn't speak for days.
13. Robert won't be ..... to finish school this year because he was absent so much.
14. No one, no matter how perfect, can ..... be right.
15. "How many times do I have to tell you to put your toys ..... after you have finished playing with them?"
16. ..... there were twenty-one pupils in the class — ten boys and eleven girls.
17. In an American house, the first floor lies directly ..... the cellar.
18. I wasn't ..... of how much I had offended him.

X. Put in the right word.

(It doesn't always begin with 'A'. Be careful!)

1. "Is it all ..... if I pay you back next week?"
2. "..... about breakfast? It's seven o'clock already, and I have to leave for work in fifteen minutes!"
3. The cook added salt ..... the water before he cooked the vegetables.
4. "Can't you wash the car tomorrow? I want to go shopping ..... afternoon."
5. The baby ducks walked ..... after another behind their mother.
6. He'll never ..... anywhere. He's too lazy.
7. When Eric returned home after four years abroad, his parents ..... him with open arms.
8. "I want to ..... your attention to a mistake at the bottom of the second page."
9. According ..... the newspaper report, it was a fight to the finish!
10. I learned to ride a bicycle ..... the age of ten.
11. No one will be admitted ..... the theatre once the performance has begun.
12. "Someone will have to answer ..... these mistakes!"
13. The new tax doesn't apply ..... owners of small businesses.

14. "Here's your order, madam. Will there be anything ..... ?"
15. My father often ..... asleep when he watches television.
16. Even if you don't agree with me, you could at ..... listen to my point of view.
17. "I don't know why you are ashamed ..... those marks. They are far above average!"
18. She was bursting with curiosity and never stopped asking .....
19. Since you have so much practical experience in these matters, I'll act ..... your advice.
20. In my opinion Steven ..... advantage of his parents.
21. "I took these pictures twenty years..... How things have changed since then!"
22. "In my opinion this car runs pretty well. After ..... it's over ten years old!"
23. "..... again will I eat there! The service was terrible!"
24. Do these figures ..... into account the increase in the cost of living?
25. "I agree ..... you. It's very useful to know English."
26. The two nations ..... an agreement to limit the development of new weapons.
27. Among other ....., I like listening to music, taking pictures and travelling.
28. The dog was friendly at first, but then all at ..... it bit me!
29. "I haven't the faintest idea. For all I ..... he could be in Africa!"
30. "You may stay as long as you wish. As ..... me, I'm going home!"
31. I'll let you know as soon as the committee arrives at a .....
32. "I'm awfully ..... that you're ill. I hope you feel better soon."
33. I wouldn't try to climb that mountain ..... anything. It's too dangerous.

Check your *answers*! *Add up* the results. Are you *above average*, *average*, or *below average*? Do you need more study? Or have you *arrived at the decision* to move *ahead*?

Key

I 1b, 2a, 3c, 4a, 5c, 6c, 7b, 8b, 9c, 10a

II 1b, 2a, 3b, 4a, 5b, 6a, 7b, 8b, 9c, 10b, 11c, 12a, 13b, 14a, 15b, 16a, 17b, 18b, 19c

III 1b, 2a, 3b, 4b, 5b, 6a, 7c, 8b, 9b

IV 1F, 2F, 3F, 4T, 5T, 6T, 7T, 8F, 9T, 10F, 11T, 12F

V 1e, 2g, 3j, 4b, 5m, 6c, 7k, 8l, 9h, 10n, 11a, 12i, 13f, 14d

VI 1e, 2f, 3a, 4b, 5d, 6c

VII 1 address, 2 action, 3 attention, 4 articles, 5 animals, 6 account, 7 adventure, 8 accident, 9 act, 10 air, 11 agreement, 12 admission, 13 application, 14 anxiety, 15 appointment, 16 age, 17 advertisements, 18 appearances, 19 advice, 20 arrangements, 21 activities, 22 art

VIII 1 add, 2 arise, 3 admit, 4 arrested, 5 admired, 6 account, 7 aimed, 8 accept, 9 acted, 10 admit, 11 amounted, 12 asked, 13 account 14 advised, 15 appoint, 16 arrange, 17 approached, 18 apply, 19 accompanied, 20 astonishes

IX 1 afraid, 2 ancient, 3 across, 4 anxious, 5 along, 6 absolute, 7 available, 8 ahead, 9 active, 10 awake, 11 against, 12 angry, 13 able, 14 always, 15 away, 16 altogether, 17 above, 18 aware

X 1 right, 2 what, 3 to, 4 this, 5 one, 6 get, 7 welcomed, 8 call, 9 to, 10 at, 11 to, 12 for, 13 to, 14 else, 15 falls, 16 least, 17 of, 18 questions, 19 on, 20 takes, 21 ago, 22 all, 23 never, 24 take, 25 with, 26 made, 27 things, 28 once, 29 know, 30 for, 31 decision, 32 sorry, 33 for

How many mistakes have you made?

	I to VI	VII to IX	X	
Excellent	0— 7	0— 6	0— 4	mistakes
Good	8—14	7—12	5— 8	mistakes
Satisfactory	15—21	13—18	9—12	mistakes
Not very good	22—35	19—30	13—16	mistakes
Weak	over 35	over 30	over 16	mistakes

B for Beginning

Beginning is difficult. One problem is that *by and large*, most words have more than one meaning. In this *book*, each exercise *brings out* one way to express an idea. *Bit by bit*, you will discover which words *belong* together!

I. What's the opposite?

1. Life *begins* at birth and
   a) continues for years.
   b) ends in death.
   c) starts with age.

2. Sugar is not *bitter;* it's
   a) sour.
   b) stiff.
   c) sweet.

3. Cities are *big;* villages are
   a) large.
   b) small.
   c) quiet.

4. I like coffee *after* a meal, not
   a) before it.
   b) besides it.
   c) between it.

5. Beethoven was *born* in 1770 and
   a) stopped in 1827.
   b) finished in 1827.
   c) died in 1827.

6. *Bad* food doesn't taste nice, but
   a) good food does.
   b) old food does.
   c) worse food does.

7. *Black* is the opposite of
   a) yellow.
   b) white.
   c) blue.

8. There were two *brothers* and three
   a) nephews in the family.
   b) sisters in the family.
   c) nieces in the family.

9. The *broken* pump could not be
   a) repaired.
   b) dropped.
   c) washed.

10. I always *go to bed* late, and
    a) stay up all night.
    b) get up early.
    c) work until morning.

11. Painters like their *best* pictures to be on display, not their
    a) famous ones.
    b) favourite ones.
    c) worst ones.

Möchten Sie regelmäßig über unser Fremdsprachenprogramm informiert werden?

Regelmäßige Informationen

Möchten Sie gerne regelmäßig über unser Fremdsprachenprogramm informiert werden? Dann kreuzen Sie bitte die entsprechende(n) Sprache(n) an und senden Sie uns die Karte mit Ihrem Namen und Ihrer Adresse zu.

Bitte informieren Sie mich regelmäßig:
(bitte ankreuzen)

☐ Arabisch
☐ Dänisch
☐ Deutsch
☐ Deutsch als Fremdsprache
☐ Englisch
☐ Französisch
☐ (Neu-)Griechisch
☐ Italienisch
☐ Niederländisch
☐ Portugiesisch
☐ Russisch
☐ Schwedisch
☐ Serbokroatisch
☐ Spanisch
☐ Türkisch

GI

Meine Adresse:

Vorname Name

Straße

PLZ, Wohnort

Bitte als
Postkarte
frankieren

An den
Ernst Klett Verlag
für Wissen und Bildung, Stuttgart
Abt. Information und Beratung
Expeditionslager
Postfach 11 70

7054 Korb

Klett

K 0424 (8/90)

12. People don't usually walk *backwards* but
    a) forwards.
    b) frontwards.
    c) behind.

13. When must I *return* the money I
    a) bought?
    b) borrowed?
    c) brought?

14. People see what happens *in front of* them, not what happens
    a) beside them.
    b) below them.
    c) behind them.

II. Which word or phrase has almost the same meaning?

1. The meeting *broke up* at eleven.
   a) began
   b) ended
   c) continued

2. Heavy snow *blocked* the road.
   a) closed
   b) cleared
   c) cleaned

3. Last winter was *bitingly cold.*
   a) rather cold
   b) extremely cold
   c) not at all cold

4. *That's none of your business.*
   a) I'll tell you all about it.
   b) That doesn't concern you.
   c) You don't own it.

5. *Besides* us, no one else is going.
   a) in spite of
   b) because of
   c) except for

6. We'll have to get together *before long!*
   a) later on
   b) very soon
   c) next year

7. *Bit by bit*, you are learning English!
   a) little by little
   b) all at once
   c) in short

8. Your remark *borders on* absolute nonsense!
   a) praises
   b) is almost
   c) encourages

9. "May I have just *a bit* of salad?"
   a) a large amount
   b) a small amount
   c) a fair amount

10. Who's *to blame for* these mistakes?
    a) in favour of
    b) responsible for
    c) excited about

11. World War II *brought about* great changes in Europe.
    a) caused
    b) prevented
    c) defeated

12. Just *bear in mind* that we haven't got much money.
    a) complain
    b) forget
    c) remember

Do your best here! You'll reach the *bottom of the page before* you know it!

III. Which choice makes sense?

1. He's really got brains.
   a) He'll never catch up.
   b) He's first in his class.
   c) He's always in the dark.

2. My radio is broken.
   a) I'm very pleased with it.
   b) It's in perfect condition.
   c) It doesn't work.

3. That book's not bad!
   a) I really enjoyed it.
   b) It was a waste of time!
   c) I never want to see it again.

4. Don't beat about the bush.
   a) I've just planted it!
   b) Keep quiet!
   c) Say what you are thinking!

5. "Where did you get that black eye?"
   a) "In a fight."
   b) "At dinner."
   c) "In the hospital."

6. I wonder what's become of her.
   a) I see her every day.
   b) She looks much better now.
   c) I haven't seen her for years.

7. We can't employ him. To begin with,
   a) he's worked here for years.
   b) he hasn't got enough experience.
   c) he's a remarkable person.

8. I can't bear him.
   a) He keeps his fingers crossed.
   b) He's my best friend.
   c) He's terribly rude.

9. We feel very bad
   a) about leaving you here alone.
   b) about helping you to get on.
   c) about your doing well.

10. I'm glad you brought that up again.
   a) It's not worth mentioning.
   b) I had forgotten about it.
   c) Mind your own business.

IV. Is it true or false?

	T	F
1. Beef comes from oxen, cows and bulls.	☐	☐
2. Plants take baths.	☐	☐
3. Bees make honey.	☐	☐
4. An insect is a bird.	☐	☐
5. Young people become old.	☐	☐
6. Bicycles have four wheels.	☐	☐
7. Bakers bake bread.	☐	☐
8. Balls are square.	☐	☐
9. Bare-footed children wear shoes.	☐	☐
10. Fish sleep in beds.	☐	☐
11. The end comes before the beginning.	☐	☐
12. Flowers have blooms.	☐	☐
13. Bells ring.	☐	☐
14. The sky is beneath my feet.	☐	☐
15. Bridges are built over rivers.	☐	☐

It's all right with us if you stop a minute to *catch your breath!*

V. Find the nouns which go together.

A. 1. brother, 2. bridge, 3. button, 4. branch, 5. bee, 6. battle, 7. beggar

a) river, b) honey, c) war, d) tree, e) shirt, f) sister, g) money

B. 8. berry, 9. beef, 10. bank, 11. band, 12. book, 13. belt, 14. beard

h) page, i) music, j) trousers, k) hair, l) cattle, m) fruit, n) money

C. 15. ball, 16. brush, 17. board, 18. broadcast, 19. belief, 20. butcher, 21. border

o) religion, p) customs, q) meat, r) lodging, s) teeth, t) radio, u) game

VI. Find the words which go together.

A.

1. bill	5. brain	9. lungs
2. bicycle	6. boat	10. fire
3. wind	7. heart	11. bell
4. water	8. bench	12. teeth

a) to sit, b) to beat, c) to ring, d) to burn, e) to pay, f) to boil, g) to blow, h) to think, i) to ride, j) to brush, k) to sail, l) to breathe

B.

13. to play	15. to press	17. to take .....
14. to blow	16. to shed	18. to read .....

m) blood, n) a book, o) ball, p) a bath, q) a button, r) a whistle

C.

19. to beat ..... the bush	22. to stay ..... bed
20. to boil ..... rage	23. to bear ..... mind
21. to burst .... tears	24. to go .... business

s) with, t) into, u) in, v) about, w) in, x) into

Did you burst out laughing because the last exercises were easy? We hate to *break the news to you, but* you'll have to *rack your brains* on the next ones!

VII. Put in the right noun.

1. The heart pumps ..... throughout the body.
2. Mountains and rivers form good natural ..... between countries.
3. We hired a good ..... to play for the dance.
4. Some ..... are so high that ships can pass beneath them.
5. During the first few months of life, a ..... depends on its mother for everything.
6. A person's ..... is determined largely by his past experiences.
7. ..... and ..... are insects with wings.
8. To keep healthy, your ..... needs good food, enough sleep and plenty of exercise.
9. I have a different ..... for each pair of trousers.
10. You can often find a good ..... at a clearance sale.
11. Wine and beer are stored in large wooden .....
12. During the violent storm last night, a ..... broke off a tree near our house and fell across the road.
13. Napoleon was defeated at the ..... of Waterloo in 1815.
14. I ran so fast that I was completely out of ..... when I reached the bus stop.
15. ..... are good building material.
16. Three factory workers were killed by the ..... at the factory yesterday afternoon.

17. That ..... is for putting on the outside lights.
18. Americans often have eggs, milk, bread with butter and jam, orange juice, and coffee or tea for .....
19. The ..... is man's thought centre.
20. Every man was once a ....., and every woman a girl.
21. Our local ..... always sells us the best joints of meat.
22. Bottles hold mostly liquids and gases, whereas ..... hold mostly solid things, including bottles.
23. Boys love to walk along high walls, trying to keep their .....
24. ..... give the body shape, and support and protect such inner organs as the heart, lungs and stomach.
25. After work on a hot day, I come home, take a ..... and then have supper with my family.
26. ..... is a favourite German drink.
27. I finally found the papers I was looking for — at the very ..... of the pile!
28. You can eat many of the small ..... which grow wild in the forest.
29. Throughout the world, children love to play .....
30. Most religions insist on the existence of a higher ....., called "God" in English.
31. On hot summer days the city's parks are full of people sitting on the ....., lying on the grass or just walking around.

VIII. Put in the right verb.

1. Once the old hotel had caught fire, it ..... down quickly.
2. "There you ..... ! I thought you were downstairs in the cellar."
3. You should ..... your teeth at least twice a day.
4. Water changes into steam when it .....
5. A modest man never .....
6. Mother always ..... all kinds of cakes for Christmas.
7. Don't ..... other people for your own mistakes.
8. At home he ..... differently from when he's with friends.
9. As soon as the noon whistle ....., the workers leave for lunch.
10. Every mother has her own ideas about how to ..... her children.
11. Dogs sometimes ..... people who they don't like.
12. When she heard that her son couldn't come home for Christmas, she ..... into tears.
13. After the battle, the dead were ..... in simple graves.
14. Mother was the first to ..... the news of grandfather's death to me.
15. I can't ..... the sight of blood.

IX. Put in the right adjective or preposition.

1. ..... men can't see.
2. In America and Great Britain eggs are sold ..... the dozen.
3. My sister Ann has dark ..... hair, but mine is .....
4. It's ..... him to talk to his servants.
5. As I stepped out of the house, the sun was so ..... that for a moment I couldn't see.
6. Even ugly people are ..... to those who love them.
7. A ..... soldier doesn't run from danger; he has the courage to stay and fight.
8. He is the only person ..... the manager who has a key.
9. Many cities are building ..... new streets to replace older narrow ones.
10. Few officials dare to introduce ..... new ideas to the public.
11. A ..... person has to organize his time carefully.

X. Put in the right word.

(It doesn't always begin with 'B'. Be careful!)

1. "Don't ..... the blame on me. It's your fault!"
2. Since our daughter had a high temperature, I ..... her to bed and called the doctor.
3. We paused several times to ..... our breath as we climbed the hill.
4. The hunter brought the lion ..... with a single shot!
5. "Mr Wilson is abroad ..... business this week."
6. In order to turn on the radio, just ..... this button.
7. The joke was so funny that we all burst out .....
8. "..... are you?" "Fine, thank you!"
9. He complained about everything. Because ..... him, no one enjoyed the trip.
10. "I beg your .....? Did you say something to me?"
11. He says that he believes ..... justice and equality, yet he's very prejudiced against certain groups of people.
12. The young boy bent ..... to tie up his shoe.
13. "..... you and me, I don't believe a ..... of it!"
14. Although T. S. Eliot was American ..... birth, he became a British citizen in 1927.
15. The thieves murdered the bank clerk in ..... blood.
16. The policeman blew his ..... and the traffic stopped.
17. Mrs. Wilson is nice, but she boasts too much ..... her son.
18. Japanese people bow ..... one another when they meet.
19. "I'd like two ..... of bread, a bag of flour and a dozen of those oranges, please."

20. The president of the club brushed ..... my objections and continued with the meeting.
21. "Back ..... a little, — you're blocking the drive!"
22. "It's all right ..... me if you listen to the radio, but could you turn it down a bit?"
23. The two men robbed the bank in broad ....., yet no one even noticed!
24. I'm going to brush ..... on my English before I go to London again!
25. This pen doesn't belong ..... me. Is it yours?
26. I ..... my best to convince her, but she wouldn't believe me.
27. Even though her parents frown on it, Susan is bent ..... becoming a doctor.
28. If you can come early, then so ..... the better.
29. These are beyond ..... the best photographs you have ever taken.
30. When the police questioned him, the man finally broke ..... and confessed.
31. "Sorry! I didn't mean to break ..... on a private conversation."
32. My wife told me about it ..... breakfast this morning. What a shame!
33. "Would you like a ..... of bread and butter with your meal?"
34. The paint was a bit scratched, but by and ..... the car was in good condition.
35. Mrs. Jones buys all her provisions ..... the local grocer.

Now check your answers. Don't *feel bad* if you made mistakes! *Bear in mind* that experience is the best teacher. *Before long*, you will understand radio *broadcasts* and be able to read *books* and newspapers!

Key

I 1b, 2c, 3b, 4a, 5c, 6a, 7b, 8b, 9a, 10b, 11c, 12a, 13b, 14c

II 1b, 2a, 3b, 4b, 5c, 6b, 7a, 8b, 9b, 10b, 11a, 12c

III 1b, 2c, 3a, 4c, 5a, 6c, 7b, 8c, 9a, 10b

IV 1T, 2F, 3T, 4F, 5T, 6F, 7T, 8F, 9F, 10F, 11F, 12T, 13T, 14F, 15T

V A. 1f, 2a, 3e, 4d, 5b, 6c, 7g — B. 8m, 9l, 10n, 11i, 12h, 13j, 14k — C. 15u, 16s, 17r, 18t, 19o, 20q, 21p

VI A. 1e, 2i, 3g, 4f, 5h, 6k, 7b, 8a, 9l, 10d, 11c, 12j — B. 13o, 14r, 15q, 16m, 17p, 18n — C. 19v, 20s, 21t/x, 22u/w, 23w/u, 24x/t

VII 1 blood, 2 borders, 3 band, 4 bridges, 5 baby, 6 behaviour, 7 beetles, bees, 8 body, 9 belt, 10 bargain, 11 barrels, 12 branch, 13 battle, 14 breath, 15 bricks, 16 blast, 17 button, 18 breakfast, 19 brain, 20 boy, 21 butcher, 22 boxes, 23 balance, 24 bones, 25 bath, 26 beer, 27 bottom, 28 berries, 29 ball, 30 being, 31 benches

VIII 1 burned, 2 are, 3 brush, 4 boils, 5 boasts, 6 bakes, 7 blame, 8 behaves, 9 blows, 10 bring up, 11 bite, 12 burst, 13 buried, 14 break, 15 bear

IX 1 blind, 2 by, 3 brown, black, 4 beneath, 5 bright, 6 beautiful, 7 brave, 8 besides, 9 broad, 10 bold, 11 busy

X 1 put, 2 put, 3 catch, 4 down, 5 on, 6 press, 7 laughing, 8 how, 9 of, 10 pardon, 11 in, 12 down, 13 between, word, 14 by, 15 cold, 16 whistle, 17 about, 18 to, 19 loaves, 20 aside, 21 up, 22 with, 23 daylight, 24 up, 25 to, 26 did, 27 on, 28 much, 29 doubt, 30 down, 31 in, 32 at, 33 slice, 34 large, 35 from

How many mistakes have you made?

	I to VI	VII to IX	X	
Excellent	0—10	0— 6	0— 3	mistakes
Good	11—20	7—12	4— 6	mistakes
Satisfactory	21—31	13—18	7—10	mistakes
Not very good	32—48	19—28	11—17	mistakes
Weak	over 48	over 28	over 17	mistakes

C for Compare

Compare life in the *city* with life in the *country*. The *city* boy knows blocks and *corners*, *chimneys*, *concerts*, *cinemas*, *commerce*, *crime*, *confusion*, *crowds* and *cars*. The *country* boy knows *cattle*, *corn*, *cows*, *calves*, *chickens*, *cotton*, *milk* and *cheese*. With words you can *compare* your experiences. Your experiences determine your *character*. *Put your cards on the table!*

I. What's the opposite?

1. I'll *throw* the ball; you
   a) conceal it.
   b) cast it.
   c) catch it.

2. Have you any *cheap* gloves? No, we have only
   a) leather ones.
   b) expensive ones.
   c) thin ones.

3. *Correct* answers are worth more than
   a) rare answers.
   b) right answers
   c) wrong answers.

4. *Careful* drivers have fewer accidents than
   a) careless ones.
   b) inferior ones.
   c) original ones.

5. In the *country*, the air is *clean*; in the
   a) mountains, it's clear.
   b) city, it's dirty.
   c) fields, it's fresh.

6. *Clever* thieves never make
   a) stupid mistakes.
   b) false charges.
   c) quick moves.

7. Farmers *cultivate* crops and then
   a) bury them.
   b) plant them.
   c) harvest them.

8. In Australia it's not *cold* in December. It's
   a) hot!
   b) rainy!
   c) mild!

9. It's very *warm* outside; come in where it's
   a) close.
   b) cool.
   c) clean.

II. Which word or phrase has almost the same meaning?

1. He won by a *close* vote.
   a) He was very popular.
   b) He gave up.
   c) He almost lost.

2. The air *is composed of* many gases.
   a) produces
   b) removes
   c) consists of

3. My aunt is a *charming* woman.
   a) rude
   b) delightful
   c) solemn

4. The new hospital was *completed* on time.
   a) finished
   b) started
   c) destroyed

5. There is only one *correct* answer.
   a) wrong
   b) false
   c) right

6. He *called on* me when I was in hospital.
   a) neglected
   b) visited
   c) shouted to

7. Hunters often wear bright *caps*.
   a) shoes
   b) glasses
   c) hats

8. *Would you care for* a cup of coffee?
   a) will you look after
   b) do you want
   c) can you make

9. The picture *concealed* a hole in the wall.
   a) hid
   b) framed
   c) made

10. How did the quarrel *come about?*
    a) end
    b) go on
    c) start

11. The church is *in the centre* of town.
    a) in the middle
    b) on the edge
    c) by the side

12. The two killers *confessed* in court.
    a) said they were guilty
    b) said they weren't guilty
    c) refused to speak

13. The post office is *close to* the station.
    a) near
    b) on top of
    c) beneath

14. Can you *take care of* this matter for me?
 a) confuse
 b) handle
 c) delay

15. My father *is in charge of* a bank.
 a) ruins
 b) rents
 c) runs

Were these last sentences *mere child's play*? Now we'll give you a *chance* to *show your colours*! As you work, some problems may *come up*, but *don't lose courage.*

III. Which choice makes sense?

1. "Keep calm!
 a) Make haste!"
 b) Don't get excited!"
 c) Shake well before using!"

2. "Come on, let's go!
 a) What are you waiting for?"
 b) There's no rush."
 c) I prefer to stand."

3. Give me a call tomorrow.
 a) I haven't got a telephone.
 b) I won't be at home.
 c) I've got the day off.

4. Road closed!
 a) Go ahead!
 b) Speed up!
 c) Do not enter!

5. That covers everything I want to tell you.
 a) Are there any questions?
 b) I'll be finished in an hour.
 c) Now I can't find anything.

6. "Can you carry this box for me?
 a) You look busy."
 b) My hands are full."
 c) I don't need any help."

7. "Make yourself comfortable.
 a) I'm sick of it."
 b) That's not worth mentioning."
 c) Would you like something to drink?"

8. If you're not satisfied with the service,
 a) climb a ladder.
 b) change clothes.
 c) make a complaint.

9. I can't go to work today—
 a) my car is in good condition.
 b) I have a bad cold.
 c) I have no complaints.

10. Go ahead — take a chance!
    a) You have nothing to lose.
    b) I've got lots more.
    c) I'd rather walk.

11. It's nothing to be concerned about —
    a) just a dangerous criminal.
    b) just a small cut.
    c) just a serious accident.

12. Pay close attention!
    a) The next sentences are important!
    b) I haven't got anything else to say.
    c) The following instructions are useless!

IV. Is it true or false?

	T	F
1. A calf is a young chicken.	☐	☒
2. Cherries are red.	☒	☐
3. Clocks tell the time.	☒	☐
4. A copy is not an original.	☐	☒
5. People sit in chairs.	☒	☐
6. Mice catch cats.	☐	☒
7. Corn grows on trees.	☐	☒
8. Cows give milk.	☒	☐
9. Curtains hang in front of windows.	☒	☐
10. Your lungs are inside your chest.	☒	☐
11. Circles have corners.	☐	☒
12. Honest people cheat. ?	☐	☐
13. Pigs climb trees.	☐	☒
14. A king wears a crown.	☒	☐
15. On a clear day it is foggy.	☐	☒
16. People wear clothes.	☒	☐
17. Cattle swim in the sea.	☐	☒
18. A captain commands a ship.	☒	☐
19. Your chin is just above your mouth.	☐	☒

Why *complain*? You're *in charge* here! We *can't command* you to do anything!

V. Find the nouns which go together.

A. 1. cheek — 2. companion — 3. case — 4. castle — 5. cat — 6. camp — 7. chest — 8. captain

a) tent, b) law, c) mouse, d) ship, e) face, f) king, g) friend, h) lungs

6 3 5 8 1 4 2 7

B. 9. chimney 10. coffee 11. club 12. current 13. curtain 14. collar 15. concert 16. calf 17. clock

i) cow, j) member, k) window, l) smoke, m) shirt, n) bean, o) electricity, p) watch, q) music

C. 18. coal 19. clothes 20. capital 21. cattle 22. cloud 23. crime 24. church 25. cottage 26. carpet

r) rain, s) floor, t) murder, u) mine, v) coat, w) farm, x) house, y) money, z) service

D. 27. class 28. chicken 29. court 30. cotton 31. commerce 32. cinema 33. clerk

aa) egg, bb) judge, cc) office, dd) school, ee) film, ff) cloth, gg) trade

VI. Find the words which go together.

A. 1. to catch ..... 2. to comb ..... 3. to climb ..... 4. to change ..... 5. to cross ..... 6. to cook .....

a) clothes, b) a meal, c) fire, d) the road, e) hair, f) a ladder

B. 7. to pay ..... 8. to cover ..... 9. to take into ..... 10. to drive ..... 11. to play .....

g) a distance, h) a car, i) cards, j) customs, k) consideration

Would you care for some nouns *for a change? Take your choice* — they're *free of charge!*

VII. Put in the right noun.

1. Law suits are handled in .....
2. People go to ..... to attend religious services.
3. A man's ..... is his moral guide.
4. Paris is the ..... of France.
5. A car which is in good ..... runs well.
6. On the farm, ... and ..... are produced from milk.
7. Christians believe that Christ died on the .....
8. Ideally wages should increase as the ..... of living rises.
9. "All aboard," called the ship's .....
10. Some people consider it ..... to keep animals locked up.
11. Mother keeps her pots and pans in the kitchen .....

12. As the storm approached, dark ..... filled the sky.
13. A ..... is a hundred years.
14. A dog makes a good ..... for a child.
15. A large ..... gathered in the street to watch the house burn down.
16. The president appointed a ..... to study the traffic problem in large cities.
17. Instead of driving to work today, I took the bus for a .....
18. A good ..... accepts his responsibilities and insists on his rights.
19. We had a very calm ..... to England this year.
20. Mountain roads have many dangerous ..... and .....
21. Some people resist ....., even if it's an improvement.
22. Grown-ups had to pay to see the film, but children were admitted free of .....
23. Practical people usually have a great deal of .....
24. Murder and robbery are serious .....
25. ..... causes a child to ask questions.
26. My uncle's son is my .....
27. ..... are a form of money: they are generally round and flat and made of metal.
28. ..... is people talking to one another.
29. A ..... does general office work, such as filling out forms, answering the telephone and taking messages.
30. One of the most unusual buildings in Germany is King Ludwig II's ..... at Neuschwanstein.
31. Bottles, barrels, boxes, baskets, cans and bags are all types of .....
32. At the ..... last night, we heard works by Dvorak, Tchaikovsky and Aaron Copland.
33. As production ..... increase, prices rise.
34. A man's ..... shows itself in what he says and does.
35. In a ..... people sleep in tents and cook out of doors.
36. A business school offers ..... in management, advertising, plant organization and many other fields which are useful for business.
37. Considering her age, my grandmother was in remarkably good ..... after the operation.
38. Just by ..... I met an old friend on the way to work this morning!
39. Many modern African nations were formerly European .....
40. At Christmas people send greetings ..... to their close friends and relatives.
41. Few things are always one .....: grass is not always green; water is not always blue; apples are not always red!
42. As it was raining, we decided to go and see a film at the local .....

43. In the evening, before I go to bed, I take my ..... off and hang them up.
44. Countries with ports along their ..... enjoy great advantages in foreign trade.
45. A ..... is like a rope, but it's made from metal rings.
46. ..... are so concerned about their own safety that they rarely fight for their beliefs.
47. It's dangerous to swim in a river which has a fast-moving .....
48. In some countries it's a common ..... to greet friends by shaking hands.
49. The police could not immediately determine the ..... of the fire.
50. A good ..... can make a restaurant famous.

VIII. Put in the right verb.

1. Roads ..... towns, cities and countries with each other.
2. Every day except Saturday and Sunday I go to work at eight and ..... home at five.
3. We had to ..... the walk because it rained.
4. People ..... all sorts of things, including cards, coins, stamps, books and records.
5. In the late eighth and early ninth centuries, Charlemagne ..... most of western Europe.
6. The last time I ..... a cold, I also developed a bad cough.
7. The captain ..... his company to attack.
8. Even today, doctors cannot ..... certain rare diseases.
9. A baby ..... when it needs food or wants attention.
10. Schubert ..... music for many of Goethe's poems.
11. When I get up in the morning, I wash, shave and then ..... my hair.
12. Before you start the test, I want to ..... your attention to certain changes in the instructions.
13. As the horses raced round the last bend, the crowd stood and ..... wildly.
14. The company was forced to ..... all salaries by five per cent in order to stay in business.
15. "Where do you ..... from?" "I'm originally from Scotland, but now I live in London."
16. As soon as I arrive home from work in the evening, I ..... my clothes, then I ring up my girl-friend and we go out for dinner.
17. Even though road conditions were bad, we ..... a great distance on the first day of our trip.
18. If you're not careful he'll ..... with you — he's not far behind you now!

19. When my grandfather died, I had to ..... my stay in Rome and return home.
20. In the spring I have my winter clothes ..... before I put them away for the summer.
21. The old box which we found in one corner of the cellar was ..... with dust; it ..... old love-letters, a few books, several broken toys and some pictures of our parents when they were younger.

Pay close attention — this concerns you: you *can* go to bed *with a clear conscience* if you *complete* the rest of the 'C's' now. *Come on, let's go!*

IX. Put in the right adjective or adverb.

1. ..... seats are the most comfortable on the train.
2. ..... cloth feels rough.
3. It is both easy and ..... to pay your bills through a bank.
4. People are less ..... of time when they enjoy their work.
5. In general, ... clothes are poorly made and wear out quickly.
6. We were very ..... to know why he had come.
7. A ..... person has faith in himself, and knows what he can and can't do.
8. Your description isn't ..... You left out several details.
9. Few things are ..... in life except for birth, death and taxes!
10. The seats in the cinema were so ..... that I fell asleep during the film!
11. "Be .....! That's a live wire!"
12. It's ..... to pull an animal's tail, even in fun.
13. "Are there any ..... cups in the kitchen? These are all dirty."
14. "Don't stand so ..... to the fire. You will burn yourself!"
15. "For heaven's sake close the door. I'm .....!"

X. Put in the right word.

(It doesn't always begin with 'C'. Be careful!)

1. "Would you care ..... a glass of orange juice with your breakfast?"
2. "Mr Black, this man claims to ..... you. Is he a friend of yours?"
3. "The final step is to connect this red wire ..... that white wire. Then your radio should work again!"
4. She lives in the large white house just ..... the corner.
5. "I hear no objections, so the ..... is carried!"
6. During the customs ..... we had to open all our luggage.
7. When Thomas joined the army, he had to have his hair .....
8. The flood water carried ..... a lot of valuable soil.
9. "As I read each name aloud, check it ..... on your list."

10. "..... me a call as soon as you arrive at the station, and I'll come for you."
11. Yesterday our dog was hit by a car when it tried to ..... the road.
12. On election day, people waited in long lines to cast their .....
13. "That's his problem. It's no concern ..... mine!"
14. The four men sat round the table playing cards and cracking .....
15. The woman in the burning house called for ....., but nobody heard her.
16. Fortunately we were able to ..... the enemy in check until we received more supplies.
17. How many people are there ..... the committee?
18. I have confidence ..... James. He has a lot of energy, and he learns quickly from his mistakes.
19. I expected to receive a raise, but instead my ..... was cut!
20. John's a good worker. You can always count ..... him to do a good job.
21. I won't climb that ..... unless you hold it steady.
22. Dry leaves and sticks catch ..... easily.
23. "..... care not to scratch this record. It's my favourite one."
24. "What ..... is your car?" "It's light blue!"
25. I've changed my ..... I'll do it for you, after all.
26. One of the two men has been charged with a serious ..... — murder.
27. "I won't be a party to that. I couldn't do it with a ..... conscience."
28. Each spring we cut all the dead branches ..... the trees in our yard.
29. I caught ..... of her for a moment as the train entered the station.
30. To the best of my knowledge, the ..... of taxes never came up during the meeting.
31. "I'll agree to help you on one ..... — that you tell me the whole truth!"
32. Some people always complain ..... the weather.

Can it be true? That covers everything! You have *completed* the 'C's'. *Check* your answers. Have you a large *collection* of right ones?

Key

I 1c, 2b, 3c, 4a, 5b, 6a, 7c, 8a, 9b
II 1c, 2c, 3b, 4a, 5c, 6b, 7c, 8b, 9a, 10c, 11a, 12a, 13a, 14b, 15c
III 1b, 2a, 3c, 4c, 5a, 6b, 7c, 8c, 9b, 10a, 11b, 12a
IV 1F, 2T, 3T, 4T, 5T, 6F, 7F, 8T, 9T, 10T, 11F, 12F, 13F, 14T, 15F, 16T, 17F, 18T, 19F

V A. 1e, 2g, 3b, 4f, 5c, 6a, 7h, 8d — B. 9l, 10n, 11j, 12o, 13k, 14m, 15q, 16i, 17p — C. 18u, 19v, 20y, 21w, 22r, 23t, 24z, 25x, 26s — D. 27dd, 28aa, 29bb, 30ff, 31gg, 32ee, 33cc

VI A. 1c, 2e, 3f, 4a, 5d, 6b — B. 7j, 8g, 9k, 10h, 11i

VII 1 court, 2 church, 3 conscience, 4 capital, 5 condition, 6 cheese, cream, 7 cross, 8 cost, 9 captain, 10 cruel, 11 cupboard, 12 clouds, 13 century, 14 companion, 15 crowd, 16 committee, 17 change, 18 citizen, 19 crossing, 20 curves, corners, 21 change, 22 charge, 23 common sense, 24 crimes, 25 curiosity, 26 cousin, 27 coins, 28 conversation, 29 clerk, 30 castle, 31 containers, 32 concert, 33 costs, 34 character, 35 camp, 36 courses, 37 condition, 38 chance, 39 colonies, 40 cards, 41 colour, 42 cinema, 43 clothes, 44 coasts, 45 chain, 46 cowards, 47 current, 48 custom, 49 cause, 50 cook

VIII 1 connect, 2 come, 3 call off, 4 collect, 5 conquered, 6 caught, 7 commanded, 8 cure, 9 cries, 10 composed, 11 comb, 12 call, 13 cheered, 14 cut, 15 come, 16 change, 17 covered, 18 catch up, 19 cut short, 20 cleaned, 21 covered, contained

IX 1 first-class, 2 coarse, 3 convenient, 4 conscious, 5 cheap, 6 curious, 7 confident, 8 complete, 9 certain, 10 comfortable, 11 careful, 12 cruel, 13 clean, 14 close, 15 cold

X 1 for, 2 know, 3 to, 4 round, 5 motion, 6 inspection, 7 cut, 8 away, 9 off, 10 give, 11 cross, 12 ballots, 13 of, 14 jokes, 15 help, 16 keep, 17 on, 18 in, 19 salary, 20 on, 21 ladder, 22 fire, 23 take, 24 colour, 25 mind, 26 crime, 27 clear, 28 off, 29 sight, 30 question, 31 condition, 32 about

How many mistakes have you made?

	I to VI	VII to IX	X	
Excellent	0—11	0—11	0— 3	mistakes
Good	12—22	12—22	4— 6	mistakes
Satisfactory	23—32	23—33	7—10	mistakes
Not very good	33—50	34—43	11—16	mistakes
Weak	over 50	over 43	over 16	mistakes

24.7.92 12 M = good+

D for Discover

Discover new words! *Develop* your vocabulary! *Down to the present day,* English has acquired words from many *different* languages. *There's no doubt about it* — this makes English exciting!

I. What's the opposite?

1. I work *during the day* and sleep
   a) until morning.
   b) at night.
   c) all afternoon.
2. "I *doubt* whether you will
   a) discover this, but ..."
   b) believe this, but ..."
   c) need this, but ..."
3. He has *a great deal* of money, but
   a) little common sense.
   b) much experience.
   c) a lot of courage.
4. Shakespeare was *born* in 1564; he
   a) directed in 1616.
   b) died in 1616.
   c) disappeared in 1616.
5. Failure *discourages;* success
   a) encourages.
   b) educates.
   c) overcomes.
6. *Difficult* exercises aren't
   a) funny!
   b) easy!
   c) essential!
7. In the Bible *God* is good;
   a) the Deal represents evil.
   b) the Devil represents evil.
   c) the Double represents evil.
8. *Safe* drivers never speed up before
   a) distant mountains.
   b) dangerous curves.
   c) dusty deserts.
9. What goes *up* must come
   a) down!
   b) due!
   c) deep!
10. *Dreams* often have their origin in
    a) knowledge.
    b) sleep.
    c) reality.
11. *Clean* clothes always become
    a) dark again.
    b) damaged again.
    c) dirty again.

12. *Life* ends in
a) depth.
b) death.
c) debt.

13. Your proposal has more *advantages* than
a) dangers.
b) disadvantages.
c) defences.

14. When *hope* is lost, there is only
a) despair.
b) defeat.
c) destruction.

II. Which word or phrase has almost the same meaning?

1. A man who is *in debt*
a) saves money.
b) owes money.
c) owns money.

2. The postman *delivered* the letter.
a) posted
b) stamped
c) brought

3. "*What can I do for you?*"
a) "May I help you?"
b) "May I interrupt you?"
c) "May I join you?"

4. Strong men can *defend* themselves.
a) provide for
b) protect
c) protest

5. I *discussed* your suggestion with Jack.
a) argued about
b) talked over
c) wondered at

6. *Due to* the weather, all flights were delayed.
a) because of
b) in spite of
c) according to

7. "*Drop me off* at the corner!"
a) put me off
b) pick me up
c) let me off

8. A friend of mine *dropped in* for a few minutes after work.
a) accidentally fell
b) came to visit
c) came about

9. *What are you driving at?*
a) What do you want to say?
b) Where do you want to go?
c) What do you want to do?

10. Children can be a pure *delight!*
    a) joke
    b) joy
    c) task

11. It's easy to *deceive* a fool.
    a) trust
    b) trick
    c) trip

12. What you say is true to a certain *degree.*
    a) temperature
    b) fever
    c) extent

Without a doubt, people who know English are *in demand* throughout the world!

III. Which choice makes sense?

1. Do come!
   a) We have plenty of room!
   b) We can't stand you!
   c) We shan't be at home!

2. It's too dark in here!
   a) Please open the window!
   b) Please turn on the light!
   c) Please keep quiet!

3. He's a good person to deal with.
   a) He loves to play games.
   b) He's completely helpless.
   c) He's extremely honest.

4. Let's drop the subject.
   a) It's very interesting.
   b) We're really making progress.
   c) There's no point in discussing it further.

5. You don't have to go into details.
   a) I need more information.
   b) I already know about it.
   c) I must know exactly what happened.

6. What's the difference!
   a) He risked his life!
   b) This is extremely important.
   c) It doesn't matter anyway.

7. Drop me a line!
   a) I'd like to hear from you!
   b) I need more rope!
   c) I'm in trouble!

8. He drives me crazy!
   a) He has just bought a new car.
   b) I'll be glad when he has gone.
   c) I think the world of him.

9. This discussion is too deep for me.
   a) I've really got brains.
   b) I can't make head or tail of it.
   c) It's beneath me.

10. He's dead tired this morning.
   a) He went to bed early.
   b) He stayed up all night.
   c) He slept like a top.

11. That's a delicate question.
   a) It's not worth mentioning.
   b) Let's ask everyone.
   c) We shouldn't discuss it here.

12. Do it without delay!
   a) It's extremely important.
   b) It doesn't matter.
   c) It can wait until tomorrow.

13. The game ended in a draw.
   a) The police had to stop the fighting.
   b) Everyone took sides.
   c) Nobody won.

14. He's completely in the dark.
   a) I wonder what's become of him.
   b) He means business.
   c) He doesn't know a thing about it.

Your success *depends on daily* work. *Take a day off* and you may forget everything. You have a *duty towards yourself* to move ahead *without delay!*

IV. Is it true or false?

	T	F
1. At noon it's dark.	☐	☐
2. Ducks love water.	☐	☐
3. The desert is cold and wet.	☐	☐
4. The postman delivers the milk.	☐	☐
5. A soldier's duty is to fight.	☐	☐
6. Dinner is the morning meal.	☐	☐
7. Daily newspapers appear weekly.	☐	☐
8. It's dangerous to drive carelessly.	☐	☐
9. Some people take delight in horrible things.	☐	☐
10. After it rains, there is a lot of dust in the air.	☐	☐
11. Interesting people are dull.	☐	☐

V. Find the nouns which go together.

A. 1. dream　　3. devil　　5. doll
   2. dress　　4. doctor　　6. desert

   a) hospital, b) toy, c) sleep, d) sand, e) evil, f) woman

B. 7. daughter
8. degree
9. dinner
10. day
11. duck
12. display

g) window, h) meal, i) son, j) water, k) temperature, l) date

VI. Find the words which go together.

A. 1. to draw .....
2. to drive .....
3. to develop .....
4. to dig .....
5. to draw .....
6. to deliver .....

a) a film, b) a speech, c) a hole, d) a picture, e) a car, f) conclusions

B. 7. to wash .....
8. to follow .....
9. to knock at .....
10. to pay .....
11. to run into .....
12. to cure .....
13. to go into .....
14. to serve .....

g) dinner, h) damages, i) details, j) the dishes, k) the door, l) directions, m) a disease, n) debt

Don't let these sentences *drive you crazy!* If you are *determined* to work *each day*, you *deserve* success. *Draw a deep breath* and continue!

VII. Put in the right noun.

1. A ..... is a toy.
2. When our first ..... was born, we named her Ann.
3. Temperature is measured in ......
4. A complete ..... consists of the month, day and year, for example: "April 23rd 1954."
5. People who can't pay their bills run into ......
6. After he had carefully considered all the facts, the judge finally came to a ......
7. Strong armies win victories, weak ones suffer ......
8. As Christmas approaches, crowds fill the streets, looking at the gifts on ..... in shop windows.
9. Prices are determined by the laws of supply and ......
10. At home my sister and I always wash the ..... after supper.
11. The ..... between Frankfurt and Paris is 580 kilometers.
12. People who talk honestly with one another learn to understand and accept the ..... between them.
13. A ..... is proof that you own a piece of property.
14. Many of Dickens' novels contain detailed ..... of life in nineteenth century England.
15. If the police hold you responsible for an accident, you must pay ......
16. The business ....., where most of the offices are, is in the centre of the town.

17. In a one way street you may only go in one . . . . . .
18. People who live in the cities sometimes feel a strong . . . . . to move to the country.
19. The storm did a great deal of . . . . . : streets were flooded, telephone lines were broken, trees were blown over and several houses were destroyed.
20. The weapons which serve a small nation for . . . . . may be useless to a more powerful nation.
21. You're most likely to get a good . . . . . on a used car if you buy it from someone you know.
22. In order to avoid danger, a river-boat captain needs to know the . . . . . of the river at all times.

Are you *dead tired* now? *Don't work yourself to death!* That would *destroy* all your good work!

VIII. Put in the right verb.

1. Ten . . . . . by two is five.
2. If a nation is attacked, it must . . . . . itself.
3. After the flood, relief supplies were . . . . . among the people.
4. I can't . . . . . any firm conclusions from the information you have given me.
5. Einstein . . . . . himself in the study of mathematics.
6. A salesman has to . . . . . with all kinds of people in his work.
7. I was . . . . . in rush hour traffic and missed my flight to New York.
8. The speaker . . . . . his final remarks to the young people at the meeting.
9. Poor people often . . . . . without things they need.
10. Balboa . . . . . the Pacific Ocean in 1513.
11. One war can . . . . . in a week the work of a thousand years.
12. After she had washed them, Mother hung up the wet clothes to . . . . . .
13. Our first results were so encouraging that we . . . . . our efforts to solve the problem.
14. You can . . . . . a picture with a pen, pencil or even a piece of chalk.
15. The Foreign Minister . . . . . a speech before a large group of representatives from various countries.
16. After his 21st birthday, the boy will be free to . . . . . of the property as he wishes.
17. I don't like to . . . . . to work in rush hour traffic, so I always leave home early.
18. Although he was at a great disadvantage from the start, he was . . . . . to succeed.

19. There wasn't a drop of wine left in the bottle — we had ..... it all!
20. Only a highly trained critic can ..... an original painting from a copy.
21. An act of courage, such as saving someone's life, ... to be rewarded.

IX. Put in the right adjective.

1. "I don't want to be like everyone else. I want to be .....!"
2. A good businessman always keeps his records ......
3. Only a good swimmer should swim in ..... water.
4. ..... objects can be easily damaged.
5. Interesting people are much more popular than ..... ones.
6. The curtains were so .... that I had to wash them twice.
7. In order to reach a decision, a court must be given ..... information about a case.

X. Put in the right word.

(It doesn't always begin with 'D'. Be careful!)

1. Just as you ..... at the door, the telephone rang!
2. The man who goes from house to house and ..... letters is called a postman.
3. "May I have the ..... dance?"
4. The people who live ..... door are good friends of ours.
5. While a soldier is ..... duty, he must obey army rules.
6. Just ..... the directions! They're printed on the box.
7. ..... a distance the man looked like my father, but when he came nearer I saw that it wasn't him.
8. There's no doubt ..... it! This glass is of very high quality.
9. My father was down ..... influenza all last week, but he feels much better now.
10. If these terms are satisfactory to you, then I'll draw ..... the agreement.
11. The ..... day I forgot to lock the front door when I left for work.
12. She's quite different ..... her brother. He's a very quiet person, but she never stops talking!
13. The teacher directed the next question ..... Thomas.
14. "While you put the food on the table, I'll ..... down to the cellar and get a bottle of wine."
15. Which shirt have you decided ..... — the woollen one or the cotton one?
16. The day was cold and clear. ..... the distance we could even see the mountains.

17. "Have you a pen with you? I want to ..... down that address."
18. "Have you a book which explains American history ..... detail?"
19. The teacher divided the pupils in the class ..... four groups.
20. Even though I was wrong, Richard ..... to my defence.
21. My father has Saturday and Sunday ..... every week.
22. We all depend ..... other people to some extent.

That will do. We've *decided* not to *delay* you a minute longer. But first, check your answers. And *don't* be *discouraged* — *in due time* your *difficulties* will *disappear!*

Key

I 1b, 2b, 3a, 4b, 5a, 6b, 7b, 8b, 9a, 10c, 11c, 12b, 13b, 14a
II 1b, 2c, 3a, 4b, 5b, 6a, 7c, 8b, 9a, 10b, 11b, 12c
III 1a, 2b, 3c, 4c, 5b, 6c, 7a, 8b, 9b, 10b, 11c, 12a, 13c, 14c
IV 1F, 2T, 3F, 4F, 5T, 6F, 7F, 8T, 9T, 10F, 11F
V A. 1c, 2f, 3e, 4a, 5b, 6d — B. 7i, 8k, 9h, 10l, 11j, 12g
VI A. 1d/f, 2e, 3a, 4c, 5d/f, 6b — B. 7j, 8l, 9k, 10h, 11n, 12m, 13i, 14g
VII 1 doll, 2 daughter, 3 degrees, 4 date, 5 debt, 6 decision, 7 defeats, 8 display, 9 demand, 10 dishes, 11 distance, 12 differences, 13 deed, 14 descriptions, 15 damages, 16 district, 17 direction, 18 desire, 19 damage, 20 defence, 21 deal, 22 depth
VIII 1 divided, 2 defend, 3 distributed, 4 draw, 5 distinguished, 6 deal, 7 delayed, 8 directed, 9 do, 10 discovered, 11 destroy, 12 dry, 13 doubled, 14 draw, 15 delivered, 16 dispose, 17 drive, 18 determined, 19 drunk, 20 distinguish, 21 deserves.
IX 1 different, 2 up-to-date, 3 deep, 4 delicate, 5 dull, 6 dirty, 7 detailed
X 1 knocked, 2 delivers, 3 next, 4 next, 5 on, 6 follow, 7 from, 8 about, 9 with, 10 up, 11 other, 12 from, 13 at, 14 go, 15 on, 16 at, 17 write, 18 in, 19 into, 20 came, 21 off, 22 on

How many mistakes have you made?

	I to VI	VII to IX	X	
Excellent	0—8	0—5	0—2	mistakes
Good	9—16	6—10	3—4	mistakes
Satisfactory	17—24	11—15	5—6	mistakes
Not very good	25—40	16—25	7—11	mistakes
Weak	over 40	over 25	over 11	mistakes

E for Experience

Every now and then, *everyone* has a fine *experience*. You are no *exception*! If you want to share this *experience* with others, you must be able to *express* yourself clearly. *Explanations*, *especially*, require *exact* words. We're *excited* about the 'E's' because here there are an *extraordinary* number of *excellent* '*experience*' words!

I. What's the opposite?

1. An *empty* box weighs less than
   a) a full one.
   b) a heavy one.
   c) a large one.

2. He's a *poor* mechanic, but an
   a) economical tailor.
   b) excellent musician.
   c) expensive merchant.

3. The opposite of *evil* is
   a) justice.
   b) good.
   c) beauty.

4. It is not *easy* to do a
   a) hard exercise,
   b) useful exercise.
   c) simple exercise.

5. Gold is *expensive*, not
   a) cheap.
   b) coarse.
   c) common.

6. The sun rises *in the morning* and sets
   a) elsewhere.
   b) in the evening.
   c) as early as possible.

7. Russia is *east* of Germany, and
   a) west of Japan.
   b) south of Denmark.
   c) north of Italy.

8. Science is the study of *cause* and
   a) experience.
   b) effect.
   c) effort.

9. I was tired, so I went to bed *early* and got up
   a) soon.
   b) late.
   c) slowly.

10. *Estimated* costs are not
    a) useful.
    b) necessary.
    c) exact.

11. I *enjoy* my work, but I
  a) don't like to work in the evenings.
  b) refuse to work in the evenings.
  c) prefer to work in the evenings.

12. Although *everyone* in the union wanted a raise,
  a) somebody wanted to go on strike.
  b) nobody wanted to go on strike.
  c) anybody wanted to go on strike.

13. *Everything* is finished —
  a) is there anything else to do?
  b) there is something else to do!
  c) there is nothing else to do!

Take it easy. Don't go to extremes. Enjoy yourself as you do these *exercises.*

II. Which word or phrase has almost the same meaning?

1. *Odds and ends* are
  a) peculiar objects.
  b) small, unimportant things.
  c) types of numbers.

2. A flood destroyed the *entire* village.
  a) hollow
  b) hole
  c) whole

3. I always *enjoy* a good beer!
  a) like
  b) refuse
  c) pour

4. Two and four *equals* six.
  a) involves
  b) makes
  c) concerns

5. Few people can *escape from* prison.
  a) get away from
  b) get into
  c) get along with

6. *To a certain extent,* I think you're right.
  a) in any event
  b) in part
  c) as a rule

7. He *expressed* his feelings quite clearly.
  a) stated
  b) understood
  c) controlled

8. I *hardly ever* eat at restaurants.
  a) always
  b) often
  c) rarely

9. *Every now and then* I visit my relatives.
   a) once upon a time
   b) once and for all
   c) once in a while

10. *In any event*, I don't want him to know about it.
   a) for the time being
   b) no matter what happens
   c) under these circumstances

III. Which choice makes sense?

1. Keep an eye on him!
   a) You can take him at his word.
   b) He's always in trouble.
   c) He needs glasses.

2. Why are you so late?
   a) I expected you hours ago.
   b) Did you leave work early?
   c) You're not very economical!

3. I always get excited
   a) when I'm angry!
   b) when I'm tired!
   c) when I'm calm!

4. We don't sell ready-made suits.
   a) We want to establish a record.
   b) You'll have to look elsewhere.
   c) Such a thing doesn't exist.

5. Excuse me for interrupting, but
   a) your speech isn't over yet.
   b) I have nothing to say.
   c) I didn't catch that last word.

6. The medicine took effect immediately—
   a) I felt better right away!
   b) it was completely useless!
   c) I'll never get well!

7. This shirt is the wrong size.
   a) May I examine it?
   b) May I exchange it?
   c) May I extend it?

Was that *a narrow escape*? Did you only just know *enough* to *edge your way through?*

IV. Is it true or false?

	T	F
1. The earth is flat.	☐	☐
2. You can see an echo.	☐	☐
3. Hens lay eggs.	☐	☐
4. Easter is a religious holiday.	☐	☐
5. Electricity is a form of energy.	☐	☐
6. The entire world speaks English.	☐	☐

	T	F
7. Enemies are friendly.	☐	☐
8. Essential things are unnecessary.	☐	☐
9. Good managers are efficient.	☐	☐
10. People work to earn a living.	☐	☐
11. France is east of Germany.	☐	☐
12. Extraordinary events happen every day.	☐	☐

V. Find the nouns which go together.

1. elbow
2. egg
3. engine
4. effect
5. entrance
6. echo
7. English
8. electricity
9. Easter
10. east
11. education

a) holiday, b) arm, c) sound, d) direction, e) school, f) car, g) wire, h) language, i) door, j) hen, k) cause

VI. Find the words which go together.

A. 1. to escape .....
2. to entertain .....
3. to estimate .....
4. to earn .....

a) a living, b) costs, c) from prison, d) guests

B. 5. ear ....
6. election .....
7. examination .....
8. eye ....

e) to test, f) to hear, g) to see, h) to vote

Explore each exercise. Look at *each* sentence carefully! *Every* word is *equally* important. Remember, words *express* ideas!

VII. Put in the right noun.

1. Daily ..... will help you to stay fit.
2. Scientists perform ..... in order to test new ideas.
3. Concerts are musical ......
4. A child's early ..... influence his future behaviour.
5. If you want to become a doctor, you will need a university ......
6. "Can't you at least make an ..... to help me out?"
7. Parents should set a good ..... to their children!
8. We hear with our ....., and see with our ......
9. There's almost always an ..... to every rule.
10. Politics can sometimes turn old friends into bitter ......
11. Good ..... always improve explanations.

12. As I reached for the bread, I accidentally hit my elbow on the ..... of the table.
13. Christians believe in the ..... of heaven and hell.
14. "In the ..... that we're attacked, I want all secret papers destroyed!"
15. The family went to great ..... for their daughter's marriage.
16. As a result of yesterday's ....., a new government was formed.
17. In the late nineteenth century, Gottlieb Daimler made great improvements in the petrol ......

You'll need all your *energy* now! The next sentences are not *easy*, but *every* word is *essential*. It will be worth the *effort!*

VIII. Put in the right verb.

1. The thieves ..... through a window and left through the front door.
2. The citizens cast ballots to ..... a new government.
3. Many firms ..... only highly-skilled workers.
4. In spite of all the evidence, the court could not ..... the man's guilt.
5. In English you can ..... a letter with either "Yours faithfully" or "Yours sincerely".
6. If you apply before next Friday, you can have your hunting permit ..... for six more months.
7. A good mathematics teacher can ..... how to solve a problem step by step.
8. In the late fifteenth century Vasco da Gama ..... the coast of Africa.
9. A doctor must first ..... a patient before he can recommend medical treatment.
10. "This shirt is too large. May I ..... it for a smaller size?"
11. The president of a country ..... official guests, such as kings, princes and foreign ministers, almost daily.
12. A young person is ..... in many ways: by his teachers at school, by discussions with his friends, through radio, television, books and newspapers.

Don't *ease up* now! *Nothing on earth* will help you *except* your own hard work. Always make an *effort* to do *even* the most difficult sentences.

IX. Put in the right adjective, adverb, or preposition.

1. ..... cars use little petrol.
2. Detailed descriptions are more ..... than general ones.
3. It's ..... that we finish the wheat harvest before the rain sets in.

4. At Christmas young children are always ..... to open their presents.
5. I would like to buy that coat, but I haven't got ..... money with me at the moment.
6. Young people usually get ..... before they get married.
7. Not many people have ..... political views.
8. Whenever we go fishing, we get up ....., eat a big breakfast, and then set out on foot for the mountains.
9. Society should offer all its members ..... opportunities for education and employment.
10. ..... for a few problems which arose at the beginning, everything went according to plan.
11. The local bank lends money on ..... terms — payments are low, and interest is reasonable.

X. Put in the right word.

(It doesn't always begin with 'E'. Be careful!)

1. "Every ..... I rang you up last night, you were out!"
2. "This belt is too short. May I exchange it ..... another one?"
3. Each of the men in the race hoped to establish a new world ......
4. I never feel ..... ease when I'm among strangers.
5. How many new countries have ..... into existence since World War II?
6. You can talk all day, but ..... on earth will change my opinion.
7. As the service ..... to an end, people began to leave the church.
8. Helen earns her ..... as a secretary in an office.
9. Even ..... William is over twenty, his mother still treats him like a child.
10. "..... it easy! There's no hurry."
11. Once the new traffic laws were ..... into effect, the accident rate in the city dropped sharply.
12. "I have applied for a job at the bank. Would you be ..... enough to write a recommendation for me?"
13. Even ..... I study all night, I still shan't know enough for the examination tomorrow morning.
14. Every once in a ..... I get up early and cook the breakfast.
15. The firm pays all my father's ..... expenses when he goes away on business.
16. The property extends from the edge of the road ..... that fence which you see in the distance.
17. Why is it sometimes difficult for parents and children to discuss their problems with each ..... ?
18. We tried to edge our ..... through the crowd in order to see the queen, but there were too many people!

Finally you've come to the *end* of the 'E's'. *Examine* your results. Are they *encouraging?* Perhaps you have *established a new record!* There is no *excuse* for anything but *exceptional* work!

Key

I 1a, 2b, 3b, 4a, 5a, 6b, 7a, 8b, 9b, 10c, 11a, 12b, 13c
II 1b, 2c, 3a, 4b, 5a, 6b, 7a, 8c, 9c, 10b
III 1b, 2a, 3a, 4b, 5c, 6a, 7b
IV 1F, 2F, 3T, 4T, 5T, 6F, 7F, 8F, 9T, 10T, 11F, 12F
V 1b, 2j, 3f, 4k, 5i, 6c, 7h, 8g, 9a, 10d, 11e
VI A. 1c, 2d, 3b, 4a — B. 5f, 6h, 7e, 8g
VII 1 exercise, 2 experiments, 3 events, 4 experiences, 5 education, 6 effort, 7 example, 8 ears, eyes, 9 exception, 10 enemies, 11 examples, 12 edge, 13 existence, 14 event, 15 expense, 16 election(s), 17 engine
VIII 1 entered, 2 elect, 3 employ, 4 establish, 5 end, 6 extended, 7 explain, 8 explored, 9 examine, 10 exchange, 11 entertains, 12 educated
IX 1 economical, 2 exact, 3 essential, 4 eager, 5 enough, 6 engaged, 7 extreme, 8 early, 9 equal, 10 except, 11 easy
X 1 time, 2 for, 3 record, 4 at, 5 come, 6 nothing, 7 came, 8 living, 9 though, 10 take, 11 put, 12 kind, 13 if, 14 while, 15 travelling, 16 to, 17 other, 18 way

How many mistakes have you made?

	I to VI	VII to IX	X	
Excellent	0— 6	0— 4	0— 1	mistakes
Good	7—12	5— 8	2— 3	mistakes
Satisfactory	13—18	9—12	4— 5	mistakes
Not very good	19—30	13—20	6— 9	mistakes
Weak	over 30	over 20	over 9	mistakes

F for Familiar

Every person is *familiar* with different things. A *farmer*, *for* example, knows his *fields*, *fences*, *flocks* and *farm* animals best. A child, however, is most *familiar* with the *faces* of his *family* and *friends*. *As for you*—you are *fast* becoming *familiar* with English! So just *for the fun of it*, learn the *following* words right away.

I. What's the opposite?

1. It's easier to *follow* than to
   a) steer.
   b) object.
   c) lead.
2. I *frequently* go shopping, but I
   a) often buy something.
   b) seldom buy anything.
   c) usually buy something.
3. My first attempt was a *failure*; my second was a
   a) record.
   b) success.
   c) trial.
4. The player *fell*, but then he
   a) got up immediately.
   b) rested for a while.
   c) turned over right away.
5. *Wise* men rarely make
   a) fine statements.
   b) funny statements.
   c) foolish statements.
6. We often *forget* unhappy experiences and
   a) remember pleasant ones.
   b) value pleasant ones.
   c) imagine pleasant ones.
7. The box was *full* of
   a) round bottles.
   b) empty bottles.
   c) heavy bottles.
8. Our cat jumped in the *front* window and then ran out the
   a) side door!
   b) back door!
   c) cellar door!
9. The *first* people to arrive were seated;
   a) the next ones had to stand.
   b) the last ones had to stand.
   c) the guilty ones had to stand.
10. When I'm busy, time goes *fast*; when I'm idle, time goes
    a) quickly.
    b) slowly.
    c) gradually.

11. In politics it's difficult to distinguish your *friends* from your
    a) acquaintances!
    b) enemies!
    c) relatives!

12. Time always moves *forwards*; it never moves
    a) upwards!
    b) afterwards!
    c) backwards!

II. Which word or phrase has almost the same meaning?

1. *Let's face the facts.*
    a) Let's avoid the truth.
    b) Let's admit the truth.
    c) Let's resist the truth.

2. Brazil is *famous for* its coffee.
    a) responsible for
    b) sorry for
    c) known for

3. *What's your favourite sport?*
    a) Are you in favour of sports?
    b) Which sport do you like best?
    c) Do you play any sports?

4. Cattle *feed on* grass.
    a) eat
    b) taste
    c) stand on

5. I can't *figure out* how much it's going to cost.
    a) pay
    b) believe
    c) determine

6. *From now on* you're on your own!
    a) up to now
    b) in the future
    c) first of all

7. *Are you familiar with* ancient history?
    a) are you well acquainted with
    b) are you curious about
    c) are you interested in

8. My father works for a large steel *firm*.
    a) union
    b) station
    c) company

9. *You're free to go.*
    a) You should leave.
    b) You may leave.
    c) You must leave.

10. Where can I *find* a good book on horses?
    a) buy
    b) read
    c) get

11. People are sometimes easy *to fool*.
    a) to trick
    b) to advise
    c) to offend

12. *He failed to turn up.*
a) He came late.
b) He didn't come.
c) He turned at the wrong corner.

13. *How do you feel about it?*
a) What's your objection to it?
b) What's your remedy for it?
c) What do you think of it?

14. Mothers *feed* their young.
a) are fond of
b) give food to
c) find fault with

15. He *flatly* denied the charges.
a) carefully
b) partly
c) absolutely

16. Can you *do me a favour*?
a) help me out
b) ask me in
c) send me away

17. Only a foolish person *makes fun of* other people!
a) takes pleasure in
b) laughs at
c) has respect for

18. He's old enough by now *to stand on his own two feet.*
a) to walk by himself
b) to earn his own living
c) to hand in his resignation

19. We were *fortunate* to have had good weather during our trip!
a) happy
b) lucky
c) likely

III. Which choice makes sense?

1. You can't fool me!
a) You're extremely clever!
b) I know you too well!
c) I'm completely in the dark!

2. Don't be angry.
a) I was making fun of you.
b) I wanted to frighten you.
c) I only said it in fun.

3. It was a fight to the finish.
a) No one gave in.
b) Both sides gave up.
c) I couldn't take sides.

4. He's fast asleep.
a) He goes to sleep quickly.
b) He's just pretending.
c) Nothing can wake him.

5. Stick to the facts.
a) Tell me exactly what happened.
b) Say it with flowers!
c) Don't go away.

6. The theatre filled up quickly.
   a) It wasn't very crowded.
   b) There was plenty of room.
   c) Soon every seat was taken.

7. May I have the floor?
   a) I want to polish it.
   b) I want to say a few words.
   c) I need more room.

8. I'm looking forward to seeing you again!
   a) I hope that we never meet again.
   b) I hope that we can get together soon.
   c) I hope that you stay out of town.

9. Don't blame me!
   a) I acted in bad faith!
   b) It's not my fault!
   c) It's my fault!

IV. Is it true or false?

		T	F
1.	Farmers work in the fields.	☐	☐
2.	Women's fashions never change.	☐	☐
3.	A frog is a fruit.	☐	☐
4.	Flour is like powder.	☐	☐
5.	Fog is wet.	☐	☐
6.	Feathers are heavy.	☐	☐
7.	People fight when they agree.	☐	☐
8.	Fish can't swim.	☐	☐
9.	Paper catches fire easily.	☐	☐
10.	Flowers have feet.	☐	☐
11.	Tomorrow is in the future.	☐	☐
12.	Foxes have fur.	☐	☐

V. Find the nouns which go together.

A.
1. fair	4. foot	7. fork
2. forest	5. factory	8. flock
3. fist	6. fashion	9. frog

a) toe, b) clothes, c) industry, d) sheep, e) trees, f) lake, g) crowds, h) hand, i) knife

B.
10. flesh	13. flower	16. fruit
11. furniture	14. flight	17. film
12. face	15. flake	18. fate

j) snow, k) stairs, l) rose, m) skin, n) fortune, o) pear, p) forehead, q) photograph, r) table

C. 19. female 20. frame 21. fish 22. fox 23. flavour 24. finger 25. fire 26. figure 27. feather

s) flame, t) hand, u) number, v) ocean, w) picture, x) hen, y) food, z) fur, aa) bird

VI. Find the words which go together.

A. 1. examination 2. colour 3. flour 4. feet 5. river 6. bird

a) to bake, b) to fail, c) to fly, d) to flow, e) to fade, f) to walk

B. 7. to make ..... 8. to find ...... 9. to form ..... 10. to use .... 11. to furnish ..... 12. to fold .... 13. to feel .... 14. to do .... 15. to go ...... 16. to fall ..... 17. to find .....

g) force, h) fishing, i) fit, j) friends, k) a blanket, l) in love, m) fault, n) out, o) a room, p) a favour, q) an opinion

Let's face the facts! English is not easy. *Quite a few times* you *won't have the faintest idea* which word is right. You may even *forget* a *few familiar* words. You may *feel fed up with it*, but *fight it out to the finish*!

VII. Put in the right noun.

1. A shy person doesn't make ..... easily.
2. I had to pay a ..... because I parked my car in a no parking zone.
3. Snow falls in .....
4. Many people are in favour of change, but are against the use of .....
5. A man who controls his ..... seldom shows his anger.
6. ..... are quick, clever animals with pointed noses and tails like brushes.
7. Where there's a thick ....., you can hardly see anything at all.
8. During a dry spell, there is a great danger of forest .....
9. In some countries people hang out the ..... on national holidays.
10. Your bones are covered with .....
11. Lamps, tables, beds and chairs are articles of .....
12. ..... enclose yards, fields and buildings.
13. A lot of people play sports for the ..... of it, not just to win.
14. Corn is good ..... for both animals and people.
15. A ..... can usually understand his son's problems, because he, too, was once a young man.
16. The forehead is the part of your ..... above the eyes.

17. People who take a lot of pictures often develop their own . . . . .
18. It's probably chance if someone tells your . . . . . correctly!
19. Your . . . . . consists of your mother, father, sisters, brothers, other relatives and you.
20. Farmers build fences around their . . . . . so that farm animals, such as cattle, sheep and horses, won't wander on to the road or on to another farmer's property.
21. There are five toes on each . . . . . and five . . . . . on each hand.
22. Depending on where you live, the . . . . . of your house may be made of sand, rock, earth or wood—it may even be covered with a carpet!

VIII. Put in the right verb.

1. Have you ever . . . . . in love?
2. Many birds . . . . . south for the winter, and north for the summer.
3. The River Rhine . . . . . into the North Sea.
4. These shoes don't . . . . . very well—they're too narrow.
5. We . . . . . our new house with comfortable modern furniture.
6. Oil will . . . . . on the surface of water.
7. I can . . . . . an honest person for his mistakes.
8. Rivers often . . . . . in the spring when the snow melts.
9. People . . . . . the unknown.
10. I was ill yesterday, but I . . . . . much better today!
11. Since I didn't speak the language, I couldn't . . . . . where to buy stamps.
12. In factories where there's danger of fire, smoking is . . . . .
13. Don't try to . . . . . that bottle open—the cap should screw off easily!
14. When I have a day off, I put on some old clothes, dig up some worms and go . . . . .
15. Although I thought that I was prepared for the examination, I . . . . . it.

IX. Put in the right adjective or adverb.

1. A . . . . . dog obeys his master.
2. Jokes aren't always . . . . .!
3. . . . . . meat can be kept for months before it is eaten.
4. . . . . . people enjoy meeting other people.
5. A good table has a . . . . . surface.
6. At . . . . . sight I didn't recognize you!
7. . . . . . cattle sell for high prices.
8. A hen is a . . . . . chicken.
9. A . . . . . person is no longer a complete stranger.
10. To keep . . . . . we need good food, fresh air and exercise.

11. Nowadays it is always possible to buy ..... vegetables—even in winter.
12. If you're ....., you may win a fortune before you're too old to enjoy it!
13. You can't be ..... to a person if you're prejudiced against him.
14. People who work too ..... often make careless mistakes.

This is your *final* chance to *finish* this lesson. *Write out* each new *word in full*!

X. Put in the right word.

(It doesn't always begin with 'F'. Be careful!)

1. "I won't be a party to that. That's ..... too far!"
2. ..... few minutes a train leaves the station.
3. "..... do you come from? You speak English quite well."
4. My brother has never been able to overcome his fear ..... the dark.
5. This suit is a bit ..... of fashion now, but I like it—and besides, I can't afford to buy a new one!
6. First of ..... we had to answer a lot of questions and then we had to wait for two hours before we were allowed to go.
7. He's ..... far the best worker in the office!
8. Roger certainly ..... a fool of himself at the party!
9. "..... for fun, let's hide behind the door and listen!"
10. Paul has such a free and ..... manner. He never worries about anything.
11. "Please write that word out ..... full. I don't know how to spell it."
12. When you're in Munich, don't fail ..... visit the English gardens!
13. "I haven't the faintest ..... where our luggage is. Let's ask about it at the information desk."
14. "You can depend on me. I'll be there tomorrow night ..... fail!"
15. "You should at least try to consider her point of view. That's ..... fair."
16. "How far ..... is the next town from here?"
17. He won't tell the truth ..... fear of losing his job.
18. ..... first I could only speak a few words of English, but now I have no difficulty with most conversations.
19. I'm very fond ..... that old chair. It's the most comfortable one in the house.
20. There aren't many roads in the mountains, so we'll have to travel either on horseback or ..... foot.
21. "I'm fed ..... with this house. Can't we move?"
22. Many cattle froze to ..... during last week's cold spell.

23. He claims that it's a new car, but as a ..... of fact it's over a year old!
24. The government changed its plans ..... the face of strong opposition from world leaders.
25. "I was so busy last night that I completely forgot ..... the concert."
26. Most men have to work full ..... in order to support their families.
27. A large crowd gathered ..... front of the town-hall.
28. I'm not angry about it. As I understand it, he ..... in good faith.

Find out if you have made any mistakes. *We'll be looking forward to seeing you again* soon!

Key

I 1c, 2b, 3b, 4a, 5c, 6a, 7b, 8b, 9b, 10b, 11b, 12c

II 1b, 2c, 3b, 4a, 5c, 6b, 7a, 8c, 9b, 10c, 11a, 12b, 13c, 14b, 15c, 16a, 17b, 18b, 19b

III 1b, 2c, 3a, 4c, 5a, 6c, 7b, 8b, 9b

IV 1T, 2F, 3F, 4T, 5T, 6F, 7F, 8F, 9T, 10F, 11T, 12T

V A. 1g, 2e, 3h, 4a, 5c, 6b, 7i, 8d, 9f — B. 10m, 11r, 12p, 13l, 14k, 15j, 16o, 17q, 18n — C. 19x, 20w, 21v, 22z, 23y, 24t, 25s, 26u, 27aa

VI A. 1b, 2e, 3a, 4f, 5d, 6c — B. 7j, 8m/n, 9q, 10g, 11o, 12k, 13i, 14p, 15h, 16l, 17n/m

VII 1 friends, 2 fine, 3 flakes, 4 force, 5 feelings, 6 foxes, 7 fog, 8 fire(s), 9 flag(s), 10 flesh, 11 furniture, 12 fences, 13 fun, 14 food, 15 father, 16 face, 17 film(s), 18 fortune, 19 family, 20 fields, 21 foot, fingers, 22 floor

VIII 1 fallen, 2 fly, 3 flows, 4 fit, 5 furnished, 6 float, 7 forgive, 8 flood, 9 fear, 10 feel, 11 find out, 12 forbidden, 13 force, 14 fishing, 15 failed

IX 1 faithful, 2 funny, 3 frozen, 4 friendly, 5 flat, 6 first, 7 fat, 8 female, 9 familiar, 10 fit, 11 fresh, 12 fortunate, 13 fair, 14 fast

X 1 going, 2 every, 3 where, 4 of, 5 out, 6 all, 7 by, 8 made, 9 just, 10 easy, 11 in, 12 to, 13 idea, 14 without, 15 only, 16 away, 17 for, 18 at, 19 of, 20 on, 21 up, 22 death, 23 matter, 24 in, 25 about, 26 time, 27 in, 28 acted

How many mistakes have you made?

	I to VI	VII to IX	X	
Excellent	0—10	0— 5	0— 3	mistakes
Good	11—20	6—10	4— 6	mistakes
Satisfactory	21—31	11—15	7— 9	mistakes
Not very good	32—48	16—25	10—14	mistakes
Weak	over 48	over 25	over 14	mistakes

G for Grow

To grow up means many things. *Girls* become women. Life becomes *give* and take, and not just *having a good time*. Some people *gain* weight. You can't play *games* in the *grass* any more. No one tells you to put your *gloves* on in winter. *Governments*, laws and rules become important. The *good-byes* and *greetings* are different. Nothing *goes without saying*!

I. What's the opposite?

1. I *got on* the bus at 10th Street and
   a) got up at 42nd Street.
   b) got off at 42nd Street.
   c) got away at 42nd Street.

2. A *great many* people play instruments, but
   a) some play them really well.
   b) very few play them really well.
   c) almost all play them really well.

3. The cat *gradually* approached the bird, then
   a) suddenly sprang towards it.
   b) carefully sprang towards it.
   c) slowly sprang towards it.

4. At first I *gained the upper hand*, but I still
   a) won the game.
   b) played the game.
   c) lost the game.

5. *Grown-ups* can learn from
   a) people!
   b) children!
   c) friends!

6. The weather has been very *good* this week, but last week it was
   a) bad.
   b) worse.
   c) better.

7. There's still *a great deal* of snow in the mountains, but there's only
   a) a load left in the valley.
   b) a little left in the valley.
   c) a lot left in the valley.

8. A coward *gives up* easily; a brave man
   a) faints.
   b) frowns.
   c) fights.

II. Which word or phrase has almost the same meaning?

1. *I get it!*
   a) It's mine!
   b) I understand!
   c) It's my turn!

2. People exchange *gifts* at Christmas.
   a) parents
   b) presents
   c) parcels

3. Did you *get* the card I sent you from Finland?
   a) post
   b) receive
   c) pick out

4. You'll have to *make good* the damage.
   a) pay for
   b) figure out
   c) estimate

5. Let's *get together* tomorrow at ten.
   a) mean
   b) meet
   c) meat

6. I've got to *get ready* for a test tomorrow morning.
   a) apply
   b) appear
   c) prepare

7. Van Gogh was a *great* Dutch painter.
   a) tall
   b) ordinary
   c) famous

8. There's a *great* difference in their ages.
   a) big
   b) certain
   c) slight

9. Let's *get rid of* these old shoes!
   a) repair
   b) try on
   c) throw away

III. Which choice makes sense?

1. This pen isn't much good.
   a) It was a bargain!
   b) It won't write!
   c) It's first-rate!

2. Go ahead!
   a) Stop working!
   b) Don't move!
   c) What are you waiting for?

3. Have a good time
   a) at the dance!
   b) in hospital!
   c) at the trial!

4. How do I get to the station?
   a) I'll meet you halfway.
   b) Go straight ahead.
   c) Reserve a seat.

5. That goes without saying.
   a) I'm glad you told me.
   b) Please repeat it.
   c) There's no need to mention it.

6. I can't get at it.
   a) It's in my pocket.
   b) Get the ladder.
   c) I don't understand.

7. Good-bye!
   a) I'll see you next week.
   b) How are you?
   c) Don't mention it!

Did the last exercise *give you a lot of trouble*? *Be on your guard!*

IV. Is it true or false?

	T	F
1. A good gun won't fire.	☐	☐
2. Grocers sell food.	☐	☐
3. Grass is green.	☐	☐
4. You wear gloves on your feet.	☐	☐
5. Glass breaks.	☐	☐
6. A German person is a German and speaks German.	☐	☐
7. Geese have feathers.	☐	☐
8. Gas is a grain.	☐	☐

V. Find the nouns which go together.

1. game
2. grain
3. gate
4. grave
5. garden
6. garage
7. gentleman
8. glass
9. grocer
10. glove
11. God

a) flower, b) death, c) glory, d) window, e) tennis, f) fence, g) wheat, h) car, i) hand, j) food, k) lady

VI. Find the words which go together.

A. 1. a game
2. a gun
3. a glove
4. a gate
5. a gift

a) to shoot, b) to give, c) to open, d) to play, e) to put on

B. 6. glass
7. grave
8. guest
9. guide

f) to visit, g) to lead, h) to bury, i) to drink

VII. Put in the right noun.

1. ..... is a heavy and valuable metal.
2. I park my car in the .....
3. A ..... of cards can be the cause of great quarrels.
4. Our daughter is a cheerful, confident ..... who has lots of friends.
5. Flowers are often placed on ..... in memory of the dead.
6. In the ..... behind our house, we grow flowers and vegetables.
7. The American plains were once covered with tall .....
8. I have a pair of ..... which I use for reading.
9. Throughout history, men have prayed to many different .....
10. A club is a ..... of people who meet regularly and who share a common interest.
11. Last year the ..... was covered with snow from December to March.
12. Unless you are an experienced mountain climber, take a ..... along with you.
13. My wife and I are expecting several ..... for dinner tonight.
14. "Hello!" and "How are you?" are common everyday .....
15. In 1849 when ..... was discovered in California, thousands of Americans rushed west.
16. The ..... of a country collects taxes, builds new schools and roads, keeps public order and represents its people in affairs with other nations.

VIII. Put in the right verb.

1. Summer was over; I had to ..... to school.
2. Never ..... up without trying!
3. Even the most friendly person cannot ..... with everyone.
4. As a child ....., each day is filled with new experiences.
5. At the week-end I often visit friends in the country, just to ..... from the city.
6. We always lock the front gate, so that our dog can't ..... of the yard.
7. I ..... from your remarks that you object to any changes in the present system.
8. I don't like my aunt—she always ..... me a lot of trouble.
9. Proud people never ..... in without a struggle.
10. It was only late summer, but it had already begun to ..... cold in the evenings.
11. As soon as I ..... in the morning, I wash and put on my clothes.
12. I didn't know the right answer, so I had to .....

IX. Put in the right adjective or adverb.

1. A tame horse can be very .....
2. A ..... person won't hesitate to give of his time and energy if the need arises.
3. ..... speaking, travel by air is more convenient than travel by ship.
4. I'm ..... you dropped in, but I'm sorry that you can't stay for dinner.
5. A man who is charged with a crime is not necessarily .....

X. Put in the right word.

(It doesn't always begin with 'G'. Be careful!)

1. Generally ....., cats are very clean animals.
2. The seeds of many plants are smaller than a single grain of .....!
3. As winter approached it grew quite ..... in the mountains.
4. The sign in the park said, "..... off the grass!"
5. People of different races and religions must learn to get ..... with one another.
6. "You had no right to give ..... those books. They belonged to me!"
7. In the forest the explorers had to guard ..... attacks from wild animals, especially at night.
8. The game went ..... even though it began to rain.
9. "This time I'm leaving ..... good! I'm never going to come back!"
10. "Let's get ..... of these old newspapers. We don't need them any more."
11. "Hurry up! He's gaining ..... us!"
12. When I threw the ball, it went ..... the fence and broke a window in our neighbour's house.
13. "Good evening, ... and gentlemen, and welcome to the show."
14. I was ..... to go swimming this afternoon, but the water was too cold.

Check your answers. Are you *gaining ground*?

Key

I 1b, 2b, 3a, 4c, 5b, 6a, 7b, 8c
II 1b, 2b, 3b, 4a, 5b, 6c, 7c, 8a, 9c
III 1b, 2c, 3a, 4b, 5c, 6b, 7a
IV 1F, 2T, 3T, 4F, 5T, 6T, 7T, 8F
V 1e, 2g, 3f, 4b, 5a, 6h, 7k, 8d, 9j, 10i, 11c
VI A. 1d, 2a, 3e, 4c, 5b — B. 6i, 7h, 8f, 9g

VII 1 gold, 2 garage, 3 game, 4 girl, 5 graves, 6 garden, 7 grass, 8 glasses, 9 gods, 10 group, 11 ground, 12 guide, 13 guests, 14 greetings, 15 gold, 16 government

VIII 1 go back, 2 give, 3 get along, 4 grows up, 5 get away, 6 get out, 7 gather, 8 gives, 9 give, 10 grow, 11 get up, 12 guess

IX 1 gentle, 2 generous, 3 generally, 4 glad, 5 guilty

X 1 speaking, 2 sand, 3 cold, 4 keep, 5 along, 6 away, 7 against, 8 on, 9 for, 10 rid, 11 on, 12 over, 13 ladies, 14 going

How many mistakes have you made?

	I to VI	VII to IX	X	
Excellent	0— 5	0— 3	0	mistakes
Good	6—10	4— 6	1	mistakes
Satisfactory	11—15	7—10	2—3	mistakes
Not very good	16—27	11—17	4—7	mistakes
Weak	over 27	over 17	over 7	mistakes

H for Happen

How many things *happen* in one day! You're *hungry* so you *have* a *hot* meal. You get a *haircut and shave.* You *happen to meet* a friend. You *hurt someone's feelings* because of something you said — but you *meant no harm by it.* You *hurry home* after a *hard* day's work. Today is your son's birthday — "*Happy Birthday!*" Tomorrow's a *holiday*, so tonight you can just take it easy *at home.*

I. What's the opposite?

1. Fire is *hot;* ice is
   a) hard.
   b) cold.
   c) solid.

2. *Take hold of* my arm and don't
   a) bend down!
   b) let go!
   c) give up!

3. Water flows *downhill*, not
   a) uphill.
   b) far away.
   c) back and forth.

4. Do you believe in *heaven* and
   a) hall?
   b) hill?
   c) hell?

5. It costs more to send a *heavy* parcel than a
   a) small one.
   b) light one.
   c) cheap one.

6. The first question was *hard*, but the second one was
   a) impossible.
   b) easy.
   c) soft.

7. Good news makes me feel *happy*, not
   a) unhealthy.
   b) tired.
   c) sad.

8. Can *hate* exist without
   a) hope?
   b) love?
   c) fear?

9. Many clothes which were once made *by hand* are now produced
   a) one at a time.
   b) by machine.
   c) at home.

II. Which word or phrase has almost the same meaning?

1. *That's over my head!*
   a) I can't reach it!
   b) I don't understand it!
   c) I won't touch it!

2. How did the accident *happen?*
   a) turn up
   b) turn out
   c) come about

3. It *hardly ever* rains in the desert.
   a) sometimes
   b) seldom
   c) often

4. Three armed men *held up* the bank.
   a) lifted
   b) robbed
   c) guarded

5. Traffic was *held up* because of an accident.
   a) delayed
   b) disturbed
   c) damaged

6. I *happened* to meet him yesterday.
   a) claimed
   b) chose
   c) chanced

7. *He's hard up for money.*
   a) He saves money.
   b) He owes money.
   c) He needs money.

8. Have we enough supplies *on hand?*
   a) available
   b) for sale
   c) under repair

9. I was at the *head* of the line.
   a) middle
   b) front
   c) end

10. You *had better* get up now or you will be late for school!
    a) may
    b) should
    c) can

11. He took his father's advice *to heart.*
    a) seriously
    b) patiently
    c) quietly

12. We must *hurry* or we'll miss the bus!
    a) leave
    b) rush
    c) wait

13. Can you *give me a hand with* this luggage?
    a) help me with
    b) provide me with
    c) present me with

Help yourself to some words! Learn them *by heart!*

III. Which choice makes sense?

1. I won't hear of it
   a) It's all right with me.
   b) Please speak louder.
   c) It's out of the question.
2. Please help yourself.
   a) There's enough food for everyone.
   b) I can't help you.
   c) There's nothing left.
3. Hurry up!
   a) Our flight leaves tomorrow!
   b) We're late already!
   c) That covers everything!
4. Don't lose heart.
   a) The worst is yet to come.
   b) I'm sure he'll come.
   c) You don't stand a chance.
5. You hurt his feelings
   a) when you respected his decision.
   b) when you made fun of his clothes.
   c) when you took his advice.
6. How do you do?
   a) Thank you, the same to you.
   b) Do as you please.
   c) I'm pleased to meet you.
7. I can't help it.
   a) My hands are tied.
   b) I'm to blame!
   c) No sooner said than done!
8. There's no hurry.
   a) Get ready at once!
   b) Make it short!
   c) We've plenty of time!
9. I couldn't make head or tail of it.
   a) I don't speak Italian.
   b) I understand French.
   c) I study German.

IV. Is it true or false?

	T	F
1. Honey is sour.	☐	☐
2. A cap is a hat.	☐	☐
3. Your brain is in your head.	☐	☐
4. A hammer is a tool.	☐	☐
5. Hungry people need food.	☐	☐
6. There are twenty-four hours in a month.	☐	☐
7. Horses eat bears.	☐	☐
8. The heel is part of your hand.	☐	☐

	T	F
9. A hundred is more than a thousand.	☐	☐
10. You can't trust an honest man!	☐	☐
11. Mountains are smaller than hills.	☐	☐

"New words! *Handle with care!*"

V. Find the nouns which go together.

1. hand	5. honey	9. heel
2. heir	6. harbour	10. ham
3. heaven	7. hammer	11. hospital
4. hundred	8. husband	

a) number, b) foot, c) wife, d) nail, e) bee, f) pig, g) fingers, h) fortune, i) hell, j) operation, k) ship

VI. Find the words which go together.

A. 1. heart 2. hill 3. handle

a) to open, b) to beat, c) to climb

B.	4. to feel	6. to dig	8. to hang up .....
	5. to hear.....	7. to harvest	9. to comb ....

d) your hair, e) wheat, f) a sound, g) happy, h) a hole, i) a picture

C.	10. to keep	13. to go	16. to wear .....
	11. to cut.....	14. to lose	
	12. to form	15. to do	

j) a habit, k) harm, l) a hat, m) heart, n) in half, o) house, p) hunting

Perhaps you've worked *for hours*, but *let's be honest* — a little study won't *harm* your *health!*

VII. Put in the right noun.

1. ..... is the study of the past.
2. There are sixty minutes in an ......
3. Two ..... make a whole.
4. A good ..... shelters boats and ships from severe storms.
5. Christmas and Easter are religious ......
6. For hundreds of years the ..... has been one of man's chief work animals.
7. Smoking is an expensive ......

8. If you become extremely ill, you may have to go to ......
9. A good ..... considers the needs of his wife and children.
10. The ..... is a strong muscle inside the chest which pumps blood round the body.
11. Ten times ten is a ......
12. We couldn't afford to stay in ....., so we camped during our trip.
13. ..... is a type of meat which comes from pigs.
14. Thousands of people gathered in the large ..... to hear the President speak.
15. Father has thrown his old socks out as they were full of ......
16. Cold is a lack of ......
17. I feel completely at home in my friend's ......
18. After a year I had to have the ..... on both shoes replaced.
19. Most towns have a ..... where local government activities take place.
20. An animal's ..... is called "fur".

If you *can't make head or tail* of a sentence, *don't lose heart*. You can *hardly* be expected to know everything.

VIII. Put in the right verb.

1. I always ..... my shirts after I've ironed them.
2. Farmers ..... corn in the summer.
3. "Can you ..... me with my French homework? I missed the lesson today."
4. Nobel Prizes ..... distinguished men and women from all over the world.
5. The plate was so hot that I could only ..... it for a few seconds.
6. The trunk was too small to ..... all my clothes.
7. People who can't ..... often learn to lip-read.
8. As he hadn't got a black suit, he decided to ..... one for the occasion.
9. Have you ever ..... something so well that you couldn't find it again?
10. My brother ..... himself when he fell off his bicycle.
11. People ..... wild animals for food and for sport.
12. I ..... that you don't get into difficulty on account of your remarks.
13. Before we sent the parcel off, we marked it "Glass! ..... with care!"
14. "If you think I'm wrong, don't ..... to tell me!"

IX. Put in the right adjective or adverb.

1. ..... people seldom fall ill.
2. People of many religions consider Jerusalem to be a ..... city.
3. A ..... person isn't proud.
4. Even if you can't swim, you should learn ..... to float.
5. Only a few buildings in the world are over a hundred stories ......
6. It's ..... for me to understand English when it's spoken fast!
7. The situation was ...... We couldn't get any more supplies.
8. Old tree trunks are often......
9. Very sick or old people often become .....; other people must then take care of them.
10. He was very ...... He took great pains to explain every detail in full.
11. Do animals experience ..... feelings such as love, pride, hate and shame?

X. Put in the right word.

(It doesn't always begin with 'H'. Be careful!)

1. "Have a ...... My brother will be here in a moment."
2. Here and ..... among the rocks we found small bunches of wild flowers.
3. Last spring I bought this winter coat in a clearance sale at half the original .....!
4. It's high ..... that this committee stopped talking and did something!
5. The police could not hold ..... the angry crowd.
6. How ..... toes have you on each foot?
7. "If we don't eat soon, I think I'll ..... of hunger!"
8. When I'm ..... home I always wear old, comfortable clothes.
9. "How ..... does that brown bread cost?"
10. "..... heavens! Our guests are here already!"
11. The beggar held ..... his hand and asked for money.
12. As Father came into the room, we all shouted, "Happy .....!" He was fifty years old.
13. "I ..... my hands of this whole affair. It's much too dangerous!"
14. The lack of rain this spring ..... great harm to the crops.
15. "During the day my wife stays at home with the baby and ..... house."
16. Last night my brother and I handed ..... programmes at the organ concert in church.
17. Susan ..... hard to be nice to my friends, but I knew that she didn't like them.
18. "I ..... no harm by the remark. I never thought that he would take it to heart."

19. "For heaven's ....., don't just stand there. Give me a hand!"
20. It's easier to ride a bicycle downhill than .....
21. In the long run, nothing can hold ..... the forces of change.
22. We were ..... holiday in Vienna when we heard the news.
23. "Please sit down. ..... yourself at home!"
24. It's ..... time that I received a raise!
25. A doctor has to be prepared to go and visit patients ..... all hours, day and night.
26. "I must go now. I'm ..... a hurry!"
27. ..... heart I know that you're right. Yet it's difficult for me to change my mind after so many years.
28. When I was a boy, I always wore clothes which had been handed ..... to me from my older brothers.

How many right answers *have you got?* Are you *highly pleased* with the results?

Key

I	1b, 2b, 3a, 4c, 5b, 6b, 7c, 8b, 9b
II	1b, 2c, 3b, 4b, 5a, 6c, 7c, 8a, 9b, 10b, 11a, 12b, 13a
III	1c, 2a, 3b, 4b, 5b, 6c, 7a, 8c, 9a
IV	1F, 2T, 3T, 4T, 5T, 6F, 7F, 8F, 9F, 10F, 11F
V	1g, 2h, 3i, 4a, 5e, 6k, 7d, 8c, 9b, 10f, 11j
VI	A. 1b, 2c, 3a — B. 4g, 5f, 6h, 7e, 8i, 9d — C. 10o, 11n, 12j, 13p, 14m, 15k, 16l
VII	1 history, 2 hour, 3 halves, 4 harbour, 5 holidays, 6 horse, 7 habit, 8 hospital, 9 husband, 10 heart, 11 hundred, 12 hotels, 13 ham, 14 hall, 15 holes, 16 heat, 17 house, 18 heels, 19 town-hall, 20 hair
VIII	1 hang up, 2 harvest, 3 help, 4 honour, 5 hold, 6 hold, 7 hear, 8 hire, 9 hidden, 10 hurt, 11 hunt, 12 hope, 13 handle, 14 hesitate
IX	1 healthy, 2 holy, 3 humble, 4 how, 5 high, 6 hard, 7 hopeless, 8 hollow, 9 helpless, 10 helpful, 11 human
X	1 seat, 2 there, 3 price, 4 time, 5 back, 6 many, 7 die, 8 at, 9 much, 10 good, 11 out, 12 birthday, 13 wash, 14 has done, 15 keeps, 16 out, 17 tried, 18 meant, 19 sake, 20 uphill, 21 back, 22 on, 23 make, 24 high, 25 at, 26 in, 27 at, 28 down

How many mistakes have you made?

	I to VI	VII to IX	X	
Excellent	0— 7	0— 4	0— 3	mistakes
Good	8—14	5— 9	4— 6	mistakes
Satisfactory	15—21	10—14	7— 9	mistakes
Not very good	22—35	15—23	10—14	mistakes
Weak	over 35	over 23	over 14	mistakes

I for Idea (with J and K)

Your *ideas* are an *important* part of you. Other people *judge* you largely from what you say. You may *know* a great deal, be *well-informed*, and have good *intentions*, but *if* you cannot express your thoughts clearly, *it* will be difficult for people to understand you. *It is to your interest* to *insist on* the correct word for each of your *ideas*!

I. What's the opposite?

1. An *idle* man is not
   a) careful.
   b) busy.
   c) lazy.
2. My mother *keeps* everything; she never
   a) throws anything away.
   b) takes care of anything.
   c) tears anything up.
3. Is the *impossible* ever
   a) practical?
   b) possible?
   c) popular?
4. You don't look *well* today. Do you feel
   a) dull?
   b) ill?
   c) sad?
5. *Kindness* is the opposite of
   a) failure.
   b) pain.
   c) cruelty.
6. The kingdom is ruled by a *king* and
   a) queen.
   b) prince.
   c) captain.
7. The *inside* is often different from the
   a) beside.
   b) outside.
   c) aside.

II. Which word or phrase has almost the same meaning?

1. Shy people are *ill at ease* among strangers.
   a) relaxed
   b) nervous
   c) friendly
2. *Just as* I opened the door, the telephone rang.
   a) although
   b) as soon as
   c) after
3. *Keep your temper!*
   a) Don't be careless!
   b) Don't be angry!
   c) Don't be modest!

4. Florence, Italy, is *known for* its art treasures.
   a) famous for
   b) worried about
   c) proud of

5. An efficient worker knows his job *inside out*.
   a) bit by bit
   b) at last
   c) thoroughly

6. "May I *introduce* Mr Brown to you?"
   a) describe
   b) present
   c) show

7. Can you *give me an idea of* what you have in mind?
   a) remember
   b) describe
   c) produce

8. Many students *joined* the film club.
   a) became members of
   b) became aware of
   c) became critics of

9. My nephew has *all kinds of* toys.
   a) a lot of fun with
   b) many types of
   c) no interest in

10. *Keep in mind* what I've told you!
    a) bear in mind
    b) never mind
    c) keep a record of

11. *I can't imagine* why he left home.
    a) I can't express
    b) I must find out
    c) I don't understand

12. *Let me know* when you're coming.
    a) warn me
    b) tell me
    c) remind me

Just imagine! English is a "*key*" which will open many "doors" to new experiences, *ideas* and *interests*!

III. Which choice makes sense?

1. You can depend on him.
   a) He can never make up his mind.
   b) He always keeps his word.
   c) He's all mixed up.

2. Danger!
   a) Go ahead!
   b) Never mind!
   c) Keep out!

3. I can't do it alone.
   a) Can you give me a hand?
   b) Can you give me a ring?
   c) Can you give me a chance?

4. It's of no importance.
   a) Don't forget about it!
   b) Don't joke about it!
   c) Don't worry about it!

5. All joking aside—
   a) the earth is flat!
   b) he thinks the world of you!
   c) never listen to reason!

6. I know about it already.
   a) It's news to me.
   b) Please explain it again.
   c) He told me yesterday.

7. That's not my job—
   a) it's my affair!
   b) it's your responsibility!
   c) it's his fault!

8. I turned the room inside out
   a) in order to set the table.
   b) in order to open the window.
   c) in order to find my keys.

Have you ever *known* a word "*inside out*"? Here's an *ideal* way *to kill some time. Interest yourself* in a single word and find out all *its* possible meanings!

IV. Is it true or false?

	T	F
1. Kind people are rude.	☐	☐
2. People always carry out their intentions.	☐	☐
3. An invention is something new.	☐	☐
4. Ice is hot!	☐	☐
5. Cooks work in kitchens.	☐	☐
6. You can't drink juice.	☐	☐
7. Lovers kiss.	☐	☐
8. Keys lock doors.	☐	☐
9. An improvement makes things better.	☐	☐
10. A good joke is funny.	☐	☐
11. Insects are very large animals.	☐	☐

V. Find the nouns which go together.

A. 1. key
2. kitchen
3. industry
4. island
5. joke
6. ink
7. justice

a) laughter, b) water, c) pen, d) machine, e) lock, f) law, g) cook

B. 8. kiss
9. judge
10. iron
11. juice
12. insect
13. instruction

h) liquid, i) fly, j) touch, k) metal, l) school, m) court

VI. Find the words which go together.

A. 1. jam 2. idea 3. job

a) to work, b) to eat, c) to conceive

B. 4. to inquire ..... 5. to be interested .. 6. to insist .....

d) on, e) in, f) about

C. 7. to kill ...... 10. to knock ..... 13. to join .....
8. to keep ..... 11. to invite .....
9. to iron ..... 12. to keep ......

g) clothes, h) a club, i) guests, j) in mind, k) time, l) at the door, m) one's word

D. 14. to get .... 16. to be ...... 18. to tie .....
15. to accept ..... 17. to play .....

n) a knot, o) an invitation, p) an instrument, q) in love, r) into difficulty

Can you do anything with the next exercises? They're *important*!

VII. Put in the right noun.

1. Steel is made from .....
2. In 1271 Marco Polo set out on a long ..... to China.
3. To the best of my ....., Bill and his wife are still in holiday.
4. When ..... melts, it becomes water.
5. Although Robert likes to play tricks on people, he can't take a ..... himself.
6. A sharp ..... cuts well.
7. ..... tastes nice on bread and butter.
8. On the way to London, we stopped at a small ....., where we had supper and stayed overnight.
9. A ..... is a precious stone.
10. The elbow is the ..... in the middle part of your arm.
11. Every sailor knows how to tie a good .....
12. She beamed with ..... as she looked down at her baby for the first time.
13. A recent study shows that crime is on the ..... in big cities.
14. The ..... is the joint in the middle part of the leg.
15. There's nothing like a dish of ..... on a hot summer's day.
16. What ..... of books do you like to read?
17. Next week's ..... will contain a special article on boats.
18. An ..... is a piece of land completely surrounded by water.
19. My pen won't write. There's no ..... in it.

20. ..... can destroy a marriage.
21. He gave me the ..... that he means business.
22. A ..... must be highly trained in law.

If you *get into difficulty, keep in mind* that very few things are really *impossible!*

VIII. Put in the right verb.

1. We ..... ten guests to the party, but only eight came.
2. Does a hunter have the right to ..... an animal just for sport?
3. I ..... at the door, but no one answered.
4. You can ..... your marks if you pay closer attention in class and take better notes.
5. Is the tax ..... in the price of this watch?
6. To ..... is to ask for information.
7. I ..... John well—he's a good friend of mine.
8. Do you ..... how to repair your own car?
9. I don't ..... anything about the history of Africa.
10. Alexander Graham Bell ..... the telephone in 1876.
11. During the game, I accidentally ..... the ball into our neighbour's garden.
12. Would you like to ..... us for dinner after the concert?
13. The world's population will probably ..... to 8,000,000,000 (eight thousand million) by the end of the century.
14. I can't ..... why she did such a foolish thing.
15. Before the trial began, the judge ..... me of my rights.
16. Things are changing so fast today that no one person can ..... up with the latest developments in every field of human activity.
17. While I was in hospital, my friends came every day to ..... me company.
18. My father ..... on talking even though I wasn't listening.
19. It's rude to ..... someone who is talking.
20. What ..... you most—sports, books, music or your studies?
21. John accidentally ..... over the lamp and broke it.
22. Before I could catch her, our cat ..... over the fence and got away!
23. The invention of the wheel, the development of the printing-press and the discovery of electricity have greatly ..... the course of history.

IX. Put in the right adjective, adverb, or preposition.

1. Oceans are ..... bodies of water.
2. An ..... person depends largely on himself.
3. ..... countries are not ruled by foreign powers; they govern themselves.

4. "Mr Martin is not ..... at the moment, but he'll be back this afternoon."
5. Can you name the months of the year ..... English?
6. Almost every machine in the factory stood ..... during the strike.
7. Are acts of cruelty ever ..... in war?
8. Under ..... working conditions, labour and management take each other's needs into consideration.
9. "Have you been waiting long?" "No, we have ..... arrived."
10. Is death ever a ..... punishment for a crime?

X. Put in the right word.

(It doesn't always begin with 'I', 'J' or 'K'. Be careful!)

1. By the end of the summer I was very much in ..... with Mary.
2. "..... into the garden. I want to show you my roses."
3. Just .....! Between 1850 and 1930 the population of the world doubled!
4. In my ....., men and women should have equal rights and opportunities.
5. Television has a great influence ..... young people today.
6. "Here, boy!" the man called to his dog in a loud .....
7. ..... if the train is only a few minutes late, we'll miss our connection in Frankfurt.
8. We decided to go for a swim instead ..... playing ball.
9. "If you get into ....., call for help."
10. Richard isn't interested ..... anything except sport!
11. As the express train sped around the sharp bend, six carriages jumped the .....
12. "Keep .....! I'm trying to talk on the telephone!"
13. "Where can I ..... information on world sports records?"
14. "Judging from ..... you say, the worst is yet to come!"
15. "..... in! The door's not locked."
16. "I hope I'm not keeping you ..... your work."
17. In order to keep dogs ..... of the garden, we put a fence around it.
18. "Are you looking for my brother? I saw him in the garden just ....."
19. "Keep ..... the right. We have to turn at the next corner."
20. I know his father by ....., but we've never actually met.
21. "Can you ..... your knee, or does it hurt too much?"
22. We arrived at the railway station early, so we had a cup of coffee just to kill .....
23. When I played that trick on John, he looked at me ..... if I were mad. He just can't ..... a joke!

24. Mr Jones insists ..... keeping the books himself. He doesn't trust anyone!
25. "You can get a plan of the building at the information ....."
26. "..... I join you?" "Of course, have a seat!"
27. The union and the management were unable to iron ..... their differences at yesterday's meeting.
28. "It's ..... your interest to be at work on time from now on."
29. "I can't solve this problem! Can you do ..... with it?"

We *invite* you to check your answers! Has your work *improved?*

Key

I 1b, 2a, 3b, 4b, 5c, 6a, 7b
II 1b, 2b, 3b, 4a, 5c, 6b, 7b, 8a, 9b, 10a, 11c, 12b
III 1b, 2c, 3a, 4c, 5b, 6c, 7b, 8c
IV 1F, 2F, 3T, 4F, 5T, 6F, 7T, 8T, 9T, 10T, 11F
V A. 1e, 2g, 3d, 4b, 5a, 6c, 7f — B. 8j, 9m, 10k, 11h, 12i, 13l
VI A. 1b, 2c, 3a — B. 4f, 5e, 6d — C. 7k, 8j/m, 9g, 10l, 11i, 12m/j, 13h — D. 14r, 15o, 16q, 17p, 18n
VII 1 iron, 2 journey, 3 knowledge, 4 ice, 5 joke, 6 knife, 7 jam, 8 inn, 9 jewel, 10 joint, 11 knot, 12 joy, 13 increase, 14 knee, 15 ice-cream, 16 kind(s), 17 issue, 18 island, 19 ink, 20 jealousy, 21 impression, 22 judge
VIII 1 invited, 2 kill, 3 knocked, 4 improve, 5 included, 6 inquire, 7 know, 8 know, 9 know, 10 invented, 11 kicked, 12 join, 13 increase, 14 imagine, 15 informed, 16 keep, 17 keep, 18 kept, 19 interrupt, 20 interests, 21 knocked, 22 jumped, 23 influenced
IX 1 immense, 2 independent, 3 independent, 4 in, 5 in, 6 idle, 7 justified, 8 ideal, 9 just, 10 just
X 1 love, 2 come, 3 imagine, 4 opinion, 5 on, 6 voice, 7 even, 8 of, 9 difficulty, 10 in, 11 rails, 12 quiet, 13 get, 14 what, 15 come, 16 from, 17 out, 18 now, 19 to, 20 sight, 21 bend, 22 time, 23 as, take, 24 on, 25 desk, 26 may, 27 out, 28 to, 29 anything

How many mistakes have you made?

	I to VI	VII to IX	X	
Excellent	0— 7	0— 5	0— 3	mistakes
Good	8—14	6—11	4— 6	mistakes
Satisfactory	15—21	12—16	7— 9	mistakes
Not very good	22—35	17—28	10—15	mistakes
Weak	over 35	over 28	over 15	mistakes

L for Love

What do you *love?* A friend? Your *little* brother or sister? Your mother or father? Everyday things, *like leaves* in the wind? A smile? *Laughter?* Just *life* in general?

I. What's the opposite?

1. Do you write with your *left* hand or your
   a) correct hand?
   b) right hand?
   c) wrong hand?

2. I never *found* the money which I
   a) lost.
   b) lent.
   c) lacked.

3. The flight *leaves* London at two and
   a) passes Frankfurt at four.
   b) arrives in Frankfurt at four.
   c) travels from Frankfurt at four.

4. You *lead the way;* I'll
   a) follow.
   b) drive.
   c) yield.

5. Do you want *a lot* of sugar in your coffee or only
   a) a load?
   b) a level?
   c) a little?

6. *Large* fish often feed on
   a) small ones.
   b) tame ones.
   c) young ones.

7. Do you wear your hair *long* or
   a) wide?
   b) natural?
   c) short?

8. Is it ever better to *lie* than to
   a) take the blame?
   b) tell the truth?
   c) tell someone's fortune?

9. The *last* day of winter comes before the
   a) longest day of spring.
   b) earliest day of spring.
   c) first day of spring.

10. *Heavy* boxes weigh more than
    a) light ones.
    b) large ones.
    c) long ones.

11. Do you prefer *light* or
    a) weak beer?
    b) dark beer?
    c) mild beer?

12. *Love* is beautiful;
    a) jealousy is ugly.
    b) hate is ugly.
    c) fear is ugly.

13. Shall we take the *early* train or the
    a) late train to Munich?
    b) local train to Munich?
    c) last train to Munich?

14. "*Hang on* tight—don't
    a) lie down!"
    b) let go!"
    c) line up!"

15. The ship was *loaded* in Hamburg and
    a) unloaded in New York.
    b) delayed in New York.
    c) sailed to New York.

16. Clothes which fit well are neither too *loose* nor too
    a) expensive.
    b) large.
    c) tight.

II. Which word or phrase has almost the same meaning?

1. I *love* to read mystery stories!
    a) generally prefer
    b) like very much
    c) usually hesitate

2. One of the prisoners is still *at large.*
    a) far away
    b) fat
    c) free

3. Six men *lost their lives in* the fire.
    a) died in
    b) escaped from
    c) put out

4. "Father will be home *in a little while.*"
    a) late
    b) afterwards
    c) soon

5. I'm *on the look out for* a good second-hand car.
    a) trying to find
    b) trying to guard
    c) trying to catch

6. *The party lasted all night long.*
    a) It ended at midnight.
    b) It began in the evening.
    c) It continued until morning.

7. The President spoke *at length* on foreign affairs.
    a) from memory
    b) in detail
    c) by and large

8. "We're alone *at last!*"
   a) at least
   b) finally
   c) for a while

9. It's *likely* that he never got your message.
   a) possible
   b) probable
   c) peculiar

10. This *land* is good for farming.
    a) soil
    b) seed
    c) grain

11. I'm *at a loss* what to do next!
    a) used to know
    b) already know
    c) don't know

12. *There's nothing like a good cup of tea!*
    a) Tea is a fine drink!
    b) Tea is a bitter drink!
    c) Tea is a popular drink!

13. Grandmother *looks after* the children during the day.
    a) takes care of
    b) takes note of
    c) puts up with

14. *David likes to play cards.*
    a) He's a good card player.
    b) He enjoys playing cards.
    c) He seldom plays cards.

15. Have you *looked into* all the possibilities?
    a) seized
    b) examined
    c) discussed

16. I *looked* everywhere *for* my glasses.
    a) called for
    b) asked for
    c) searched for

III. Which choice makes sense?

1. Try your luck!
   a) You don't stand a chance!
   b) You might as well give up!
   c) Maybe you'll win something!

2. Roger is interested in law.
   a) He wants to become a judge.
   b) He wants to become a doctor.
   c) He wants to become a butcher.

3. This will lead to nothing.
   a) We've almost succeeded!
   b) Let's try something else.
   c) It's worth the trouble.

4. You don't look well today.
   a) Do you need glasses?
   b) Have you got a cold?
   c) Does your hair need washing?

5. Look out for the cars
   a) when you travel by train.
   b) when there's no traffic.
   c) when you cross the street.
6. So long!
   a) I'll see you later.
   b) How do you do?
   c) Don't mention it!
7. "Have you got a light?"
   a) "This is too heavy."
   b) "That house is on fire!"
   c) "No, I don't smoke."
8. That money won't last long.
   a) He'll put it in the bank.
   b) He'll spend it right away.
   c) He'll hide it in a safe place.
9. If you don't understand a word,
   a) look at it!
   b) look it over!
   c) look it up!
10. Don't leave anything out!
    a) I'm not in the least interested.
    b) I want to know everything.
    c) I don't care about it.
11. Leave it to me!
    a) It's none of my business!
    b) I'll take care of it.
    c) I can't do anything with it!
12. There isn't any food left!
    a) We ate it all!
    b) There's plenty more!
    c) It's all right!
13. Don't speak in such a low voice.
    a) You're hurting my ears.
    b) Everyone can hear you.
    c) I can't hear you.
14. Good luck!
    a) I hope you win.
    b) I hope you lose.
    c) I hope you fail.
15. I'm looking forward to seeing you.
    a) I'm very busy right now.
    b) When can we get together?
    c) Don't stand behind me!

IV. Is it true or false?

	T	F
1. Lamps give light.	☐	☐
2. Lions are weak animals.	☐	☐
3. Letters come in the post.	☐	☐
4. Lakes are larger than oceans.	☐	☐
5. All lines are straight.	☐	☐

	T	F
6. Lazy people like to work.	☐	☐
7. Leather is a liquid.	☐	☐
8. Libraries sell books.	☐	☐
9. Lunch is a large evening meal.	☐	☐
10. We breathe with our lungs.	☐	☐
11. Lies are true.	☐	☐

Do your level best! We can *lend you a hand* from time to time, but in the *long* run everything *depends largely upon* you.

V. Find the nouns which go together.

A.
1. lungs
2. lake
3. lock
4. lunch
5. life
6. leaf
7. lamp

a) water, b) meal, c) light, d) chest, e) tree, f) death, g) key

B.
8. lips
9. lady
10. leather
11. library
12. lion
13. love
14. law

h) hate, i) animal, j) books, k) order, l) mouth, m) woman, n) skin

VI. Find the words which go together.

A.
1. fog
2. student
3. lips
4. ear
5. liquid
6. labour

a) to pour, b) to lift, c) to listen, d) to learn, e) to kiss, f) to work

B.
7. to light .....
8. to lead .....
9. to lift ....
10. to laugh .....
11. to lend .....
12. to leave .....

g) the way, h) at a joke, i) a hand, j) a cigarette, k) alone, l) a finger

C.
13. to climb .....
14. to be ....
15. to speak .....
16. to give ......
17. to make .....
18. to write .....

m) a language, n) a living, o) lessons, p) a letter, q) a ladder, r) lucky

Did the *last* exercises give you *a lot of* trouble? Don't *lose* courage! When you have finished this book, you will never *be at a loss for* words!

VII. Put in the right noun.

1. Some trees lose their ..... in the autumn.
2. Most shoes are made of .....
3. "Good .....! I hope that everything turns out all right."
4. The ..... of a society govern the behaviour of its members.
5. Each ..... in my ancient history book deals with a different civilization.
6. Is there ..... after death?
7. If you can't find the books you need here, go to the main .....
8. I have to read a ..... of books before the examinations begin.
9. She wasn't in the ..... interested in what I was saying.
10. The ..... is a member of the cat family.
11. There's a ..... to how much pain a person can bear.
12. My father makes a ..... by selling furniture.
13. The boys went fishing in the .....
14. Water, juice, coffee, tea, wine, beer and milk are all .....
15. Jane speaks two foreign .....: French and Spanish.
16. Galileo's experiments in the late sixteenth and early seventeenth centuries brought to ..... new information concerning the laws of weight and motion.
17. I looked in several shops but I couldn't find any trousers in my .....
18. Doctor Clark's studies are on a ..... with the best in the field of medicine today.
19. Confidence, determination and an understanding of people are among the most important qualities of a good .....
20. Is it possible to have many interests and yet live a simple .....?

VIII. Put in the right verb.

1. Don't ..... against the wall—I've just painted it!
2. I like to ..... to popular music.
3. The bank refused to ..... me enough money to buy a car.
4. The telephone book ..... names, addresses and telephone numbers.
5. An honest man won't .....; he'll always try to tell the truth.
6. I asked the bus driver to ..... me off at the next street corner.
7. Although the sun shone all morning, late in the afternoon it started to ..... like rain.
8. When you finish an examination, ... it over carefully before you hand it in.
9. A shy person ..... confidence.
10. My grandfather never thought that he would ..... to see man travel to the moon.

11. Can you ..... at your own mistakes?
12. Although I like to be with my friends, sometimes I just want to be ..... alone.
13. Don't forget to ..... up the office before you leave tonight.
14. "You don't look well. Perhaps you should ..... for a while."
15. My father won't ..... me go swimming in the river because the current is too fast.
16. Bright students ..... fast.
17. How do you ..... this book?
18. The sack of potatoes was so heavy that I couldn't ..... it off the ground!
19. A lack of education may ..... your chances of getting a good job.
20. If you know how to ask for directions in English, you won't ..... when you're in London.

Don't *lay* this book *aside* now! There isn't much *left* to be done!

IX. Put in the right adjective or adverb.

1. When we arrived at the theatre, there were no tickets ..... for the play.
2. "Please turn down the radio. It's too .....!"
3. A second-hand car costs ..... money than a new one.
4. The Golden Gate Bridge in San Francisco is over 1280 metres (4200 feet) .....
5. Since I needed money, I took the job even though the wages were .....
6. I hope it rains soon. I've never seen the river this .....
7. We were ..... to escape alive from the burning ship!
8. ..... people like to take it easy, even when they're at work!
9. What is the weather ..... in Norway during the summer?
10. Turn ..... at the next corner, then go straight ahead.
11. The radio is a good source for the ..... news.
12. When you are ..... in the forest, every tree looks the same.

X. Put in the right word.

(It doesn't always begin with 'L'. Be careful!)

1. "I'll do my level ..... to help you out, but I can't work wonders!"
2. The boy leaned ..... as he sped downhill on his bicycle.
3. Two people ..... their lives in road accidents last week-end.
4. "Look ..... the pictures in this book! Aren't the colours beautiful?"
5. The plants died for lack ..... water.
6. Suddenly the path ended. We had lost our .....!

7. "I've tried everything. I'm ..... a loss what to do next."
8. Mother laid the ..... and then called the family to dinner.
9. No one in the crowd lifted a ..... to help the old woman with her heavy bags.
10. Always keep your money and valuable papers under lock and .....
11. "Why have you been so nervous ..... late? Is anything wrong?"
12. The judge turned to the young man and said, "You're ..... liberty to go now."
13. Little ..... little the snow covered the ground until everything was white.
14. Mrs White ..... music lessons at her home in the evenings.
15. "Don't lay the ..... on me! I didn't do it."
16. "There's a telephone ..... the left of the stairs."
17. ..... law all citizens must pay taxes.
18. "William, leave the dog .....! He wants to sleep."
19. "What line is your father .....?" "He's in the building trade."
20. ..... or later I'll learn the truth. It's merely a matter of time.
21. "You could ..... least have tried to be polite!"
22. When I was single I could manage with less, but I can't live ..... this salary now!
23. "Don't let the dog .....—he's covered in mud!"
24. At about nine o'clock the ..... lifted and the sun shone on the wet fields and trees.
25. How many names are there ..... the list?
26. "Don't lie ..... me! I saw you hit him!"
27. "What a wonderful surprise! I'm completely ..... a loss for words!"
28. "Let me ..... when your train is due to arrive. I'll meet you at the station."
29. "Do you know what? — I can't find the keys. We're locked .....!"
30. When Mr Smith died, no one laid ..... to his property.
31. The thieves may have entered through the garage, but it's ..... likely that they came in through the window.

At last you can *look up* the answers! *Good luck!*

Key

I	**1b, 2a, 3b, 4a, 5c, 6a, 7c, 8b, 9c, 10a, 11b, 12b, 13a, 14b, 15a, 16c**
II	**1b, 2c, 3a, 4c, 5a, 6c, 7b, 8b, 9b, 10a, 11c, 12a, 13a, 14b, 15b, 16c**
III	**1c, 2a, 3b, 4b, 5c, 6a, 7c, 8b, 9c, 10b, 11b, 12a, 13c, 14a, 15b**
IV	**1T, 2F, 3T, 4F, 5F, 6F, 7F, 8F, 9F, 10T, 11F**
V	**A. 1d, 2a, 3g, 4b, 5f, 6e, 7c — B. 8l, 9m, 10n, 11j, 12i, 13h, 14k**

VI A. 1b, 2d, 3e, 4c, 5a, 6f — B. 7j, 8g, 9l, 10h, 11i, 12k — C. 13q, 14r, 15m, 16o, 17n, 18p

VII 1 leaves, 2 leather, 3 luck, 4 laws, 5 lesson, 6 life, 7 library, 8 lot, 9 least, 10 lion, 11 limit, 12 living, 13 lake, 14 liquids, 15 languages, 16 light, 17 length, 18 level, 19 leader, 20 life

VIII 1 lean, 2 listen, 3 lend, 4 lists, 5 lie, 6 let, 7 look, 8 look, 9 lacks, 10 live, 11 laugh, 12 left, 13 lock, 14 lie down, 15 let, 16 learn, 17 like, 18 lift, 19 limit, 20 get lost

IX 1 left, 2 loud, 3 less, 4 long, 5 low, 6 low, 7 lucky, 8 lazy, 9 like, 10 left, 11 latest, 12 lost

X 1 best, 2 forward, 3 lost, 4 at, 5 of, 6 way, 7 at, 8 table, 9 finger, 10 key, 11 of, 12 at, 13 by, 14 gives, 15 blame, 16 to, 17 by, 18 alone, 19 in, 20 sooner, 21 at, 22 on, 23 in, 24 fog, 25 on, 26 to, 27 at, 28 know, 29 out, 30 claim, 31 more

How many mistakes have you made?

	I to VI	VII to IX	X	
Excellent	0— 9	0— 5	0— 2	mistakes
Good	10—18	6—10	4— 6	mistakes
Satisfactory	19—28	11—15	7— 9	mistakes
Not very good	29—45	16—26	10—15	mistakes
Weak	over 45	over 26	over 15	mistakes

M for Mail

An *air-mail* letter from a friend! She's *getting married!* A brief *message* from your *mother:* "*What's the matter?* Why haven't we heard from you?" *By mistake*, someone else's parcel! A local *merchant* announces a sale. But *mostly*, just bills. *What more could you want* from one *morning's mail?*

I. What's the opposite?

1. The cup fell and *broke*. I couldn't
   a) match it!
   b) mend it!
   c) move it!
2. The pond *froze* in November, and the ice didn't
   a) mix until April.
   b) mend until April.
   c) melt until April.
3. Who are your favourite *male* and
   a) female singers?
   b) young singers?
   c) popular singers?
4. *Modern* societies developed from
   a) ancient civilizations.
   b) mysterious origins.
   c) humble beginnings.
5. Do you hold *moderate* or
   a) reasonable political views?
   b) popular political views?
   c) extreme political views?
6. *Many* paintings were on display but only
   a) a few of them won prizes.
   b) the best of them won prizes.
   c) two of them won prizes.
7. Have you ever slept from *midnight* until
   a) afternoon?
   b) noon?
   c) evening?
8. The winters here used to be *severe;* now they're quite
   a) modest.
   b) mild.
   c) merry.
9. Have you ever disappointed your *mother* or
   a) nephew?
   b) father?
   c) brother?
10. How many *men* understand
    a) women?
    b) children?
    c) youth?

You don't need *muscles* for this book. You need brains!

II. Which word or phrase has almost the same meaning?

1. *Make the most of it!*
   a) Make use of it!
   b) Make the best of it!
   c) Make off with it!

2. He'll be here *at any moment.*
   a) much later
   b) very soon
   c) sometime or other

3. *Does this poem make sense to you?*
   a) Do you understand it?
   b) Do you like it?
   c) Do you remember it?

4. Farmers work hard *from morning to night.*
   a) during the day
   b) all day long
   c) daily

5. I'll do it *this minute!*
   a) immediately
   b) in good time
   c) as soon as possible

6. *That's mine!*
   a) Leave it to me!
   b) It refers to me!
   c) It belongs to me!

7. His remarks weren't *meant* for the press.
   a) prepared
   b) reserved
   c) intended

8. "I can saddle the horse *by myself!*"
   a) without any pay
   b) without any help
   c) without any risk

9. *That may be so.*
   a) It is possible.
   b) It is natural.
   c) It is unusual.

10. *How much are these cherries?*
    a) How big are they?
    b) What do they cost?
    c) How many are there?

11. I visit Jack *once in a blue moon.*
    a) once a month
    b) very seldom
    c) at night

12. Have you *mastered* your own language yet?
    a) forgotten
    b) taught
    c) thoroughly learned

13. There you are *mistaken!*
    a) wrong
    b) right
    c) mad

14. *My parents mean a lot to me.*
   a) I complain about them.
   b) I care about them.
   c) They are cruel to me.

15. I can't *make up my mind* what to do!
   a) discuss
   b) describe
   c) decide

16. *Do you mind* if I smoke?
   a) will it disturb you
   b) will it delight you
   c) will it disappoint you

III. Which choice makes sense?

1. He has no manners.
   a) He's very polite.
   b) He's very rude.
   c) He's very foolish.

2. I learned the passage by heart.
   a) Now I can say it from memory.
   b) Now I'm all mixed up.
   c) Now it doesn't make sense to me.

3. What does this word mean?
   a) I can't spell it.
   b) I don't understand it.
   c) I can't pronounce it.

4. Never mind!
   a) I've already finished!
   b) I still need help!
   c) I'm in great danger!

5. They live from hand to mouth.
   a) They don't make much money.
   b) They eat all the time.
   c) They have no manners.

6. He lives beyond his means.
   a) He's extremely wealthy.
   b) He spends more than he can afford.
   c) He's said to be rich.

7. John changes his mind all the time.
   a) That speaks in his favour.
   b) He has a great deal of common sense.
   c) You can never depend on him.

8. He'll never make it.
   a) He's too lazy.
   b) He's quite successful.
   c) He's very lucky.

Do you feel up to the mark? Make up your mind to learn ten new words each day. *You'll make it.*

IV. Is it true or false?

		T	F
1.	Doctors practise medicine.	☐	☐
2.	People never make mistakes.	☐	☐
3.	Monkeys are clever animals.	☐	☐
4.	Air mail is sent by train.	☐	☐
5.	The moon is smaller than the earth.	☐	☐
6.	Cats like to eat mice.	☐	☐
7.	Soldiers learn how to march.	☐	☐
8.	A mechanic uses tools.	☐	☐
9.	You have muscles in your arms and legs.	☐	☐
10.	Snow melts in cold weather.	☐	☐
11.	Modest people boast a lot.	☐	☐
12.	A minute is part of a second.	☐	☐
13.	Temperature is measured in miles.	☐	☐

In the next exercises *we are willing to meet you halfway.* We have supplied the questions and the answers—but you have to *make the choices! Does that meet with your approval?*

V. Find the nouns which go together.

A. 1. murder 2. manager 3. male 4. mile 5. mouth 6. mouse 7. map 8. material

a) firm, b) cloth, c) crime, d) direction, e) man, f) distance, g) animal, h) tongue

B. 9. minister 10. Mr 11. milk 12. market 13. muscle 14. moon 15. month 16. match

i) organ, j) May, k) priest, l) Mrs, m) cow, n) merchant, o) fire, p) sun

C. 17. meadow 18. mind 19. mine 20. minute 21. meat 22. mercy 23. men

q) memory, r) women, s) time, t) grass, u) kindness, v) gold, w) beef

VI. Find the words which go together.

A. 1. to get ..... 2. to have ..... 3. to live .....

a) from hand to mouth, b) in mind, c) married

B. 4. to solve ...... 7. to operate ..... 10. to make up ....
5. to change ..... 8. to climb .... 11. to spend ....
6. to hold .... 9. to have ....

d) a mystery, e) a machine, f) one's mind, g) a mountain, h) a meeting, i) money, j) no manners, k) one's mind

C. 12. to meet ..... 14. to manage ..... 16. to make .....
13. to melt ..... 15. to miss ....

l) the bus, m) money, n) butter, o) a deadline, p) a business

VII. Put in the right noun.

1. The ..... is a type of church service.
2. There are twelve ..... in a year.
3. There are sixty ..... in an hour.
4. Gold, silver, steel, iron and tin are all .....
5. The doctor gave me some ..... for my cough.
6. You can buy fresh eggs, fruit and vegetables every day at the local .....
7. A ..... is a government official.
8. ..... and noon are twelve hours apart.
9. Sigmund Freud explored and wrote about the ..... of dreams.
10. The ..... of Richard Wagner is grand and powerful.
11. Last week-end, while I was in the country, it rained and my car got stuck in the .....
12. ..... are personal standards of right and wrong.
13. Breakfast, lunch and supper are the three main ..... of the day.
14. Many words have several ..... For example, you can win or lose a ....., and you can also light your cigarette with a .....!
15. You eat and talk with your ..... A river flows into the sea at its .....
16. Two ..... of our band were sick, so we couldn't play at the dance.
17. Even in time of war, is cruelty ever justified as a ..... to an end?
18. The stone is in the ..... of the fruit.
19. We had to sail the boat back to the land, as the ..... broke down.
20. The ..... of a ship often makes passengers sick.
21. My grandmother has a remarkably good ..... She remembers quite clearly how people lived fifty years ago.
22. Your wife rang up just now. She left a ..... for you.
23. An act of ..... is an act of kindness.
24. "I've changed my ..... I've decided to take your advice."
25. The government took ..... to control the cost of living.
26. A good road ..... shows cities, towns, bridges, rivers, lakes, and forests.
27. My brother makes his living as a worker in a large paper-.....

It doesn't matter if *you're all mixed up at the moment.* After all, you learn from your *mistakes!*

VIII. Put in the right verb.

1. William and Susan love one another and are getting ..... soon.
2. Members of the press have to ..... deadlines every day!
3. We couldn't ..... into our new house until we had sold the old one.
4. "I ..... we adjourn." "I second the motion."
5. There was so much traffic that I only just ..... to get to work on time this morning.
6. I'll ..... you at the station at six.
7. Words are ..... up of letters.
8. A painter very often has to ..... his paint in order to get a certain colour.
9. I was deeply ..... by the story which the poor old man told me.
10. "Miss Brown, I would like to introduce you to my father, Mr Williams." "Pleased to ..... you!"
11. "You can't wear that tie with that shirt. The colours don't .....!"
12. I'll need a ruler in order to ..... the length of these lines.
13. He didn't go into detail. He just ..... that he wasn't satisfied with the committee's decision.
14. When we moved to the city, I ..... the fresh air, sounds and smells of the country.

IX. Put in the right adjective.

1. A cock is a ..... chicken.
2. "My watch is .....—I can't find it anywhere!"
3. A good outline contains only the ..... ideas of a paper or report.
4. "..... Christmas and a Happy New Year!"
5. Nothing excites me more than a good ..... story!
6. "That is ..... coat—this one is yours!"
7. When he started to call me names, I became so ..... that I lost my temper.
8. Much ..... music seems "out of tune" to many people!

X. Put in the right word.

(It doesn't always begin with 'M'. Be careful!)

1. "Mark my .....! She'll marry him yet!"
2. The bus can carry forty passengers ..... most.

3. ..... and ..... Brown have been married for fifty years!
4. "I'll repeat the instructions ..... more; then you're on your own!"
5. "May I ..... you for a glass of water? I'm thirsty."
6. On Mondays mother spends most of the ..... washing and ironing clothes.
7. "..... you very much for the advice. I'll certainly keep it in mind."
8. "What's the .....? Why are you crying?"
9. The club ..... a special meeting yesterday evening in order to elect a new president.
10. Of course we ..... the deadline! As a matter of ..... we were finished two hours early!
11. A few people complained about the band, but for the most ..... everyone seemed to enjoy the party.
12. "A few details may have slipped my mind, but that's more or ..... what happened."
13. It was so dark that we could hardly make ..... the house numbers.
14. While we were in Munich we had time for either a play or a concert, but not for both. It was a difficult ..... to make!
15. "Who's there?" "It's .....! I'm home early today."
16. He wrote that poem ..... memory of his brother, who died in the war.
17. "This watch is no good at all. I have a ..... mind to take it back to the shop!"
18. Your report was excellent. There were a few small mistakes, but they aren't ..... mentioning."
19. My uncle has never ..... much money as a farmer, but he certainly enjoys his work.
20. "I couldn't make any ..... of his explanation. I'm even more confused now."
21. "Please take a seat. Mr White will be here ..... a moment."
22. A new family has just moved ..... next door. I can't wait to meet them!
23. The car has sold well ever since it was first ..... on the market two years ago.
24. Nowadays people are well informed of world events ..... means of television, radio and the newspapers.
25. I was ..... moved as I listened to her speak. How much she had suffered!
26. When the workers threatened to strike, the management decided to meet their .....
27. "This skirt only cost half ..... much as that one, yet it's much nicer!"

Check your answers. Did you *make the most of* the *material* in this lesson?

Key

I 1b, 2c, 3a, 4a, 5c, 6a, 7b, 8b, 9b, 10a
II 1b, 2b, 3a, 4b, 5a, 6c, 7c, 8b, 9a, 10b, 11b, 12c, 13a, 14b, 15c, 16a
III 1b, 2a, 3b, 4a, 5a, 6b, 7c, 8a
IV 1T, 2F, 3T, 4F, 5T, 6T, 7T, 8T, 9T, 10F, 11F, 12F, 13F
V A. 1c, 2a, 3e, 4f, 5h, 6g, 7d, 8b — B. 9k, 10l, 11m, 12n, 13i, 14p, 15j, 16o— C. 17t, 18q, 19v, 20s, 21w, 22u, 23r
VI A. 1c, 2b, 3a — B. 4d, 5f/k, 6h, 7e, 8g, 9j, 10f/k, 11i — C. 12o, 13n, 14p, 15l, 16m
VII 1 mass, 2 months, 3 minutes, 4 metals, 5 medicine, 6 market, 7 minister, 8 midnight, 9 meaning, 10 music, 11 mud, 12 morals, 13 meals, 14 meanings, match, match, 15 mouth, mouth, 16 members, 17 means, 18 middle, 19 motor, 20 motion/movement, 21 memory, 22 message 23 mercy, 24 mind, 25 measures, 26 map, 27 mill
VIII 1 married, 2 meet, 3 move, 4 move, 5 managed, 6 meet, 7 made, 8 mix, 9 moved, 10 meet, 11 match, 12 measure, 13 mentioned, 14 missed
IX 1 male, 2 missing, 3 main, 4 merry, 5 mystery, 6 my, 7 mad, 8 modern
X 1 words, 2 at, 3 Mr, Mrs, 4 once, 5 trouble, 6 day, 7 thank, 8 matter, 9 held, 10 met, fact, 11 part, 12 less, 13 out, 14 choice, 15 me, 16 in, 17 good, 18 worth, 19 made, 20 sense, 21 in, 22 in, 23 put, 24 by, 25 deeply, 26 demands, 27 as

How many mistakes have you made?

	I to VI	VII to IX	X	
Excellent	0— 8	0— 5	0— 2	mistakes
Good	9—17	6—10	3— 5	mistakes
Satisfactory	18—26	11—15	6— 8	mistakes
Not very good	27—43	16—25	9—13	mistakes
Weak	over 43	over 25	over 13	mistakes

Taking Stock

Now you are about halfway through the book, which is a good time to stop for a minute and see what progress you have made over the last few weeks, and whether you can be satisfied with your results.

Letter A	I—VI	VII—IX	X .....
Letter B	I—VI	VII—IX	X .....
Letter C	I—VI	VII—IX	X .....
Letter D	I—VI	VII—IX	X .....
Letter E	I—VI	VII—IX	X .....
Letter F	I—VI	VII—IX	X .....
Letter G	I—VI	VII—IX	X .....
Letter H	I—VI	VII—IX	X .....
Letters IJK	I—VI	VII—IX	X .....
Letter L	I—VI	VII—IX	X .....
Letter M	I—VI	VII—IX	X .....

You see, now you know exactly where you stand. Of course, you mustn't forget that you are doing well if your results stay the same. Remember, too, that by now you need less time for each exercise than you did at first. That is also a sign of your progress.

If your results for Exercises I—VI are good, you have a well-developed understanding of the language.

Exercises VII—IX, however, are more important. You mustn't be content if you had "not very good" more than five times for these. That shows that you don't know enough words by heart, and to speak English you need words!

Exercise X tests whether your use of the language is idiomatically correct. You mustn't be content with less than "good" for this exercise.

N for Necessary

By now you have learned *a number of necessary* words. You know the *names* of many things. You can read *newspaper* articles, and discuss the latest *news* with your *neighbours*. *Nevertheless*, you *need* more practice. *Note* each *new* expression. *In a nutshell*, "practice makes perfect!"

I. What's the opposite?

1. I *never* drive to work. I
   a) seldom walk.
   b) always walk.
   c) often walk.

2. The two brothers are as different as *day* and
   a) noon!
   b) night!
   c) nature!

3. Few people prefer a *foreign* country to their
   a) next door neighbours.
   b) national customs.
   c) native land.

4. *None* of the songs were familiar, but I liked
   a) most of them.
   b) all of them.
   c) some of them.

5. If *nothing* changes, then
   a) everything stays the same.
   b) anything stays the same.
   c) something stays the same.

II. Which word or phrase has almost the same meaning?

1. *Did you have a nice time?*
   a) Did you stay long?
   b) Did you fit in well?
   c) Did you enjoy yourself?

2. *Nearly all* telegrams are short.
   a) a lot of
   b) almost all
   c) only a few

3. Is the bus station *near here?*
   a) close by
   b) far away
   c) straight ahead

4. I sat *next to* my niece at dinner.
   a) behind
   b) beyond
   c) beside

III. Which choice makes sense?

1. A person usually gives notice
   a) before he changes jobs.
   b) before he lets things slide.
   c) before he applies for a job.
2. We made all the preparations for nothing.
   a) The meeting was a success.
   b) The meeting was called off.
   c) We won the match!
3. It's not your turn.
   a) I'm not in line.
   b) I'm nearby.
   c) I'm next.
4. This saw is no good!
   a) It's made to order!
   b) It's not sharp enough!
   c) It's out of tune!
5. Take note of the following details—
   a) they're not worth mentioning!
   b) they're important!
   c) they will lead to nothing!

What next? Just follow your nose until further notice!

IV. Is it true or false?

	T	F
1. Nobody has two noses.	☐	☐
2. The sun shines at night.	☐	☐
3. Many nuts taste good.	☐	☐
4. Nervous people never worry.	☐	☐
5. Noon is at midnight.	☐	☐
6. A city is larger than a neighbourhood.	☐	☐
7. Nowadays man can travel to the moon!	☐	☐

V. Find the nouns which go together.

1. nail
2. nest
3. needle
4. nut
5. nurse
6. nephew

a) niece, b) screw, c) thread, d) bird, e) hammer, f) doctor

VI. Find the words which go together.

1. net
2. nose
3. news
4. needle
5. numbers

a) to sew, b) to add, c) to fish, d) to smell, e) to report

VII. Put in the right noun.

1. Birds build ..... out of dry grass, leaves and branches.
2. We count with .....
3. The ..... supports the head.
4. Although Picasso is a ..... of Spain, he has spent most of his life in France.
5. Two ..... helped the doctor perform the operation.
6. Everyone likes to hear good .....
7. My ..... is my brother's son; my ..... is my brother's daughter.
8. ..... never makes sense.
9. Trees, birds und flowers are all part of .....
10. A good way to keep up with current events is to read the ..... daily.
11. Italy first became a ..... in 1870.
12. ..... are used to fasten boards together.
13. I recognized his face, but I couldn't remember his .....!
14. Some trees have leaves; others have .....
15. "Did you know that Mr Young retired last week?" "Why, no. That's ..... to me!"

VIII. Put in the right verb.

1. Can you ..... all the days of the week in English?
2. Neglected children ..... love.
3. The road ..... considerably as we approached the mountain pass.
4. Dogs make good guards because they ..... slight movements and noises.
5. Your body ..... not only food and water, but also exercise and rest.

IX. Put in the right adjective or adverb.

1. ..... people are seldom at ease.
2. Fresh foods have a more ..... flavour than food in tins.
3. Canada is ..... of the United States.
4. He was standing ..... me—I could hear every word he said.
5. Your ..... tongue is the language you learned to speak as a child.
6. We had quite a ..... holiday, although the weather wasn't very good.
7. Defence, foreign trade agreements and elections are matters of ..... interest.

X. Put in the right word.

(It doesn't always begin with 'N'. Be careful!)

1. ..... now on I'm going to study English for an hour every day.
2. Soldiers and policemen must be ready for duty at a ..... notice.
3. Every house ..... the neighbourhood has a fence around it.
4. Never ..... will I buy a cheap shirt. The colours always fade!
5. If need ..... I'll take the train, but I would rather drive.
6. ..... nature she's a quiet, gentle person.
7. "Tell me what Mary said!" "No, I won't. It's none of your .....!"
8. Have you ever stayed up ..... night to prepare for an examination?
9. Before the manager left the firm, he ..... a month's notice.
10. ..... a number of people asked questions after the speech.
11. ..... night I woke up in the middle of a strange dream.
12. When he ..... me names, I lost my temper.
13. After the flood, many people were ..... need of food and shelter.

Are you having a nice time? You've finished with the 'N's' now. Perhaps *you're in need of* a good *night's* rest!

Key

I 1b, 2b, 3c, 4b, 5a
II 1c, 2b, 3a, 4c
III 1a, 2b, 3c, 4b, 5b
IV 1T, 2F, 3T, 4F, 5F, 6T, 7T
V 1e, 2d, 3c, 4b, 5f, 6a
VI 1c, 2d, 3c, 4a, 5b
VII 1 nests, 2 numbers, 3 neck, 4 native, 5 nurses, 6 news, 7 nephew, niece, 8 nonsense, 9, nature, 10 newspaper, 11 nation, 12 nails, 13 name, 14 needles, 15 news
VIII 1 name, 2 need, 3 narrowed, 4 notice, 5 needs
IX 1 nervous, 2 natural, 3 north, 4 near/next to, 5 native, 6 nice, 7 national
X 1 from, 2 moment's, 3 in, 4 again, 5 be, 6 by, 7 business, 8 all, 9 gave, 10 quite, 11 last, 12 called, 13 in

How many mistakes have you made?

	I to VI	VII to IX	X	
Excellent	0—3	0—2	1	mistakes
Good	4—6	3—5	2	mistakes
Satisfactory	7—10	6—8	3	mistakes
Not very good	11—16	9—13	4—6	mistakes
Weak	over 16	over 13	over 6	mistakes

O for Opinion

You need to understand even the most *ordinary* words extremely well if you intend to express your *opinions* clearly in a foreign language. *Otherwise, once in a while* you may say the *opposite* of what you mean. *On occasion* someone might even *take offence* at your remarks! *Seize every opportunity* to improve your English, so that you will be able to reply confidently when someone asks, "*What's your opinion?*"

I. What's the opposite?

1. The shops *open* at nine in the morning and
   a) turn off at six in the evening.
   b) give up at six in the evening.
   c) close at six in the evening.

2. After work I *took off* my suit and
   a) put on some comfortable clothes.
   b) ironed a clean shirt.
   c) tried on my new trousers.

3. I *paid back* the money which I
   a) owned.
   b) owed.
   c) offered.

4. From the *outside*, can you always know what's
   a) included?
   b) intended?
   c) inside?

5. If you *offer* me the right position, I'll
   a) accept it.
   b) consider it.
   c) discuss it.

6. Last year I traded in my *old* car for a
   a) fast one.
   b) new one.
   c) used one.

II. Which word or phrase has almost the same meaning?

1. The show *was over* at eleven.
   a) continued
   b) ended
   c) started

2. Do you know how to *operate* an electric saw?
   a) steer
   b) use
   c) repair

3. What's your *occupation?*
   a) job
   b) address
   c) proposal

4. *Our television is out of order.*
   a) It doesn't work.
   b) It has been ordered.
   c) It's out of stock.

5. I have spoken with him *on several occasions.*
   a) a few times
   b) in no time
   c) only once

6. They're in love with *one another.*
   a) everybody
   b) each other
   c) someone else

7. *What's your opinion?*
   a) What are you thinking about?
   b) Are you by my side?
   c) How do you feel about this?

8. Can you come *at once?*
   a) this time
   b) right away
   c) for a while

9. I *ought to* write home tonight.
   a) may
   b) should
   c) must

10. *Hands off!*
   a) Don't push!
   b) Don't let go!
   c) Don't touch!

III. Which choice makes sense?

1. Mr Wells is out of town at the moment.
   a) He feels fine.
   b) He's on holiday.
   c) He's all mixed up.

2. Why don't you stay overnight?
   a) There's nowhere to sleep.
   b) Our flat is very small.
   c) We have plenty of room.

3. Tomorrow is my day off,
   a) so I can't stay up late!
   b) so don't wake me up early!
   c) so I have to go to work!

4. He's on his own now.
   a) He depends on his parents.
   b) He's just got married.
   c) He doesn't live at home any longer.

5. That's out of the question!
   a) Let's talk it over.
   b) I won't consider it.
   c) It goes without saying.

6. There's no need to take offence!
   a) I can't stand you any longer.
   b) We're out of danger.
   c) I meant no harm by it.

7. While my brother was at the university,
   a) I slept out of doors!
   b) I had a room of my own!
   c) I had a day off!

8. He's well off.
   a) He's out of work.
   b) He's got a good job.
   c) He lives from hand to mouth.

IV. Is it true or false?

		T	F
1.	Operations are performed in hospitals.	☐	☐
2.	The ocean is dry.	☐	☐
3.	A farmer works out of doors.	☐	☐
4.	Windows are openings in walls.	☐	☐
5.	Oranges are orange.	☐	☐
6.	Secretaries work in offices.	☐	☐
7.	It is not polite to offend people.	☐	☐
8.	Every person has his own opinions.	☐	☐
9.	Oxen are small, weak animals.	☐	☐

V. Find the nouns which go together.

1. oak
2. orange
3. office
4. ox
5. ocean
6. organ
7. officer
8. offence

a) captain, b) music, c) water, d) tree, e) animal, f) law, g) desk, h) fruit

VI. Find the words which go together.

A. 1. to obey .....
2. to offer .....
3. to oil ....
4. to observe .....
5. to owe ....
6. to overcome ...
7. to own .....
8. to open .....

a) the stars, b) the window, c) an order, d) a difficulty, e) property, f) resistance, g) a machine, h) money

B. 9. to take advantage of...
10. to play .....
11. to be .....
12. to take ...
13. to be ...
14. to put...

i) out of order, j) into operation, k) on one's own, l) the organ, m) an opportunity, n) offence

Don't take offence when someone corrects you. *Seize the opportunity* to learn from your mistakes!

VII. Put in the right noun.

1. Murder is a criminal .....
2. In the army the ..... give the orders.
3. People exchange greetings with one another on special ....., like Christmas.
4. Whenever you take a long trip by car, check the ..... frequently!
5. The Atlantic ..... lies between North America and Europe.
6. The ..... is a musical instrument which is often played in church.
7. "We haven't any ..... in your line of work—you'll have to look elsewhere."
8. The ..... of "opposition" is "agreement".
9. Once the new machines were put into ....., fewer men were needed.
10. "I'm of the ..... that we need a new hospital now!"
11. The study of the moon may help us to discover more about the earth's .....
12. The ..... of an object is determined by its shape.
13. The prisoners escaped through an ..... in the wall.

VIII. Put in the right verb.

1. "We haven't any yellow paint in stock, but we can ..... some for you."
2. Before you write a paper, you should first ..... your thoughts carefully!
3. When a man is in debt, he ..... money.
4. The children couldn't wait to ..... their Christmas presents.
5. If you ..... the motion, vote against it!
6. Knowledge helps man to ..... fear.
7. After the war the defeated countries were ..... by foreign powers.
8. Should a man ..... every order which he is given?
9. Anything which you ....., such as land, a house, a radio or a car, is your property.
10. The thief ..... no resistance when the police arrested him.

IX. Put in the right adjective, adverb, or preposition.

1. East and west are ..... directions.
2. ..... wood is valued for its strength.
3. You can hear news, music and weather reports ..... the radio.

4. When the play was ....., we went to a small restaurant for a cup of coffee.
5. If you can't give me the ..... letter, please can I have a copy of it?
6. On the ..... side of the street all the house numbers are even.
7. The bicycle badly needed painting, but ..... it was in quite good condition.
8. According to ..... reports, ten soldiers were killed in action last week.
9. Something which seems ..... to you may seem quite special to another person.
10. "Would you repeat that ..... more? I didn't catch the last word."
11. At first I didn't like him at all, but after we'd talked for a while I had to change my ..... opinion of him.
12. In some countries you will receive a glass ..... water with your meal whenever you eat in a restaurant.

X. Put in the right word.

(It doesn't always begin with 'O'. Be careful!)

1. "Well, I'm .....! I'll see you next week!"
2. There's always a guard on ..... at the prison entrance.
3. Most of the stores in town are open ..... nine to six every day except Sunday.
4. ..... or other we'll make it!
5. I'll have to borrow some money from the bank ..... order to buy the car.
6. The men who are at present ..... office were elected two years ago.
7. "I'm sick of hearing the same excuses over and over .....!"
8. "I don't agree with you. ..... my opinion, that's going too far."
9. Is it true that once upon a ..... there was no life of any sort on the earth?
10. ..... order of the chief of police, no one may park in that street.
11. ..... what day do you plan to leave?
12. Make sure that you water the plant every day or ..... it may die!
13. "Ladies and Gentlemen, I should like to ..... this opportunity to thank all of you for your support during the election."
14. When the bear saw us it turned and ran in the opposite .....
15. I'm saving my money. One ..... I hope to have my own car.
16. ..... over the world people prayed for an end to the war.
17. "I prefer a job where I can work out of ..... rather than in an office."
18. "Do you remember Paul Smith?" "Why, yes, ... yesterday I saw his picture in the paper."

19. Once in a ..... my father smokes a cigarette instead of his pipe.
20. "I'm telling you once and for .....—don't be late again!"

The lesson is *over! We have no objections* if you want to look up the answers now!

Key

I 1c, 2a, 3b, 4c, 5a, 6b
II 1b, 2b, 3a, 4a, 5a, 6b, 7c, 8b, 9b, 10c
III 1b, 2c, 3b, 4c, 5b, 6c, 7b, 8b
IV 1T, 2F, 3T, 4T, 5T, 6T, 7T, 8T, 9F
V 1d, 2h, 3g, 4e, 5c, 6b, 7a, 8f
VI A. 1c, 2f, 3g, 4a, 5h, 6d, 7e, 8b — B. 9m, 10l, 11i/k, 12n, 13k/i, 14j
VII 1 offence, 2 officers, 3 occasions, 4 oil, 5 ocean, 6 organ, 7 openings, 8 opposite, 9 operation, 10 opinion, 11 origin, 12 outline, 13 opening
VIII 1 order, 2 organize, 3 owes, 4 open, 5 oppose, 6 overcome, 7 occupied, 8 obey, 9 own, 10 offered
IX 1 opposite, 2 oak, 3 on, 4 over, 5 original, 6 opposite, 7 otherwise, 8 official, 9 ordinary, 10 once, 11 original, 12 of
X 1 off, 2 duty, 3 from, 4 somehow, 5 in, 6 in, 7 again, 8 in, 9 time, 10 by, 11 on, 12 else, 13 take, 14 direction, 15 day, 16 all, 17 doors, 18 only, 19 while, 20 all

How many mistakes have you made?

	I to VI	VII to IX	X	
Excellent	0— 5	0— 3	0— 2	mistakes
Good	6—11	4— 7	3— 4	mistakes
Satisfactory	12—16	8—11	5— 6	mistakes
Not very good	17—28	12—18	7—10	mistakes
Weak	over 28	over 18	over 10	mistakes

P for Practical (with Q)

Something which is *practical* is useful and *possible. Patience*, for example, is a *practical personal* quality which will often help you to *solve a problem* or to *keep a promise. People* can be *practical*, too. A *practical person* tries to examine all *possibilities* before he makes a decision. Is he *in a position* to act, or is the matter *beyond his power?* What's your *point of view?* Do you *take pride in* being *practical?*

I. What's the opposite?

1. Does every *question* have
   a) a request?
   b) an answer?
   c) a purpose?
2. Everyone was *present* at the meeting; no one was
   a) abroad.
   b) absent.
   c) around.
3. Can you *pick* me *up* at seven and
   a) drop me off near the library?
   b) take me to the library?
   c) drive me past the library?
4. The *past* was once the
   a) presence.
   b) present.
   c) president.
5. During the *war*, people thought that
   a) peace would never come.
   b) pardon would never come.
   c) protest would never come.
6. I expected John to *keep his promise*, but he
   a) kept the secret.
   b) gave me trouble.
   c) broke his word.
7. Do you read *quickly* or
   a) poorly?
   b) slowly?
   c) carefully?
8. She *took off* her skirt and
   a) put up a dress.
   b) took on a dress.
   c) put on a dress.
9. People do not always behave *in private* as they behave
   a) in public!
   b) on holiday!
   c) on the phone!
10. After I had *put down* the newspaper I
    a) looked for a book.
    b) read a book.
    c) picked up a book.

11. A successful business operates at a *profit*, not at
    a) a gain.
    b) a loss.
    c) a disadvantage.

12. Have you ever been *punished* when you should have been
    a) rewarded?
    b) forgiven?
    c) blamed?

13. *Poor* people can afford less comfort than
    a) employed people.
    b) rich people.
    c) young people.

14. I *accidentally* hurt her feelings. I didn't do it
    a) to no purpose!
    b) in person!
    c) on purpose!

15. Before we *put up* the new curtains, we
    a) wore out the old ones.
    b) took down the old ones.
    c) threw away the old ones.

16. You *pull* from the front and I'll
    a) kick from behind!
    b) jump from behind!
    c) push from behind!

Brushes and *paint* are the *painter's* tools. *Pen*, *pencil* and *paper* are the *poet's* tools. What are the tools of your *profession?*

II. Which word or phrase has almost the same meaning?

1. *Pardon?*
    a) What did you see?
    b) What did you say?
    c) What did you start?

2. *Pardon me!* Have you got a light?
    a) Excuse me!
    b) Help me!
    c) Tell me!

3. *I would prefer to leave.*
    a) I would rather leave.
    b) I would probably leave.
    c) I would never leave.

4. Did you take many *pictures* on your trip?
    a) presents
    b) provisions
    c) photographs

5. "Please *pass* the potatoes."
    a) serve
    b) hand me
    c) bake

6. Bill *polishes* his shoes every other day.
    a) shines
    b) signs
    c) soils

7. Are you *prepared for* the test?
a) afraid of
b) ready for
c) nervous about

8. Miss White has fifteen *pupils* in her class.
a) boys
b) people
c) students

9. Two prisoners of war were *put to death.*
a) killed
b) punished
c) caught

10. What is the *proper* way to set the table?
a) practical
b) usual
c) correct

11. A *perfect* answer is
a) beside the point.
b) completely right.
c) quite original.

12. Gold is a *precious* metal!
a) delicate
b) heavy
c) valuable

13. The President appointed a new man to fill the *post.*
a) profession
b) position
c) possession

14. What is your *position on* the tax issue?
a) opinion on
b) objection to
c) complaint about

15. Grandfather *passed away* last night.
a) resigned
b) returned
c) died

16. This photograph is *particularly* interesting!
a) rather
b) moderately
c) especially

17. If you study hard I'm sure that you'll *pull through.*
a) make up
b) make it
c) make off

18. Is it possible to *put an end to* war?
a) stop
b) step up
c) spread

19. He has *plenty of* spare time.
a) very little
b) enough
c) a lot of

20. *I have no preference.*
a) It means a lot to me.
b) It's all the same to me.
c) I am very particular.

21. *Keep this private!*
a) Keep in touch!
b) Don't tell anyone!
c) Everyone should know!

22. Our tent offered little *protection* from the cold.
a) comfort
b) shelter
c) surface

23. My brother works in a steel *plant.*
a) office
b) building
c) factory

24. I am very *pleased* with my new job!
a) satisfied
b) busy
c) unhappy

25. *What is the price of that plough?*
a) How well does it work?
b) How much does it cost?
c) How do you operate it?

26. I'd like to *propose* something new.
a) suggest
b) suppose
c) invent

May we *pass on* to you a good *piece of advice?* Even if you are *quick at learning*, *pay* close *attention* to each new word. Otherwise, *it's quite possible* that you will make some *painful* mistakes. That's *the plain truth!*

III. Which choice makes sense?

1. My father has great presence of mind.
a) He's well informed.
b) He never goes to pieces.
c) He has a good memory.

2. I won't be a party to that.
a) I think it's wrong.
b) I think it's justified.
c) I think it's urgent.

3. "Wet paint!
a) Hold on!"
b) Don't touch!"
c) Try it!"

4. My tooth hurt,
a) so I had it polished.
b) so I had it pushed.
c) so I had it pulled.

5. "We'll have to be quiet.
   a) Nobody's around!"
   b) The baby's asleep!"
   c) Everybody's up!"
6. I felt completely out of place at the party.
   a) I wasn't dressed properly.
   b) I forgot about it.
   c) I arrived on time!
7. This pencil will serve the purpose.
   a) It's broken.
   b) It won't do.
   c) I don't need a pen.
8. When winter set in,
   a) it got quite cold.
   b) the temperature rose.
   c) all the flowers blossomed.
9. He's not really asleep.
   a) He's peculiar.
   b) He's just pretending.
   c) That's beyond his power.
10. "Don't push!
   a) Hurry up!"
   b) Keep in line!"
   c) Move along!"
11. "You look rather pale.
   a) Let's play ball!"
   b) Do you feel faint?"
   c) Do you want to go swimming?"
12. He's very particular.
   a) He only eats certain foods.
   b) He loves to cook.
   c) He doesn't eat enough.
13. It's out of the question.
   a) I won't hear of it!
   b) Of course I agree to it!
   c) It's the only possible answer!
14. "It's pretty much the same here.
   a) Nothing looks familiar."
   b) Something seems different."
   c) Nothing has changed."
15. I couldn't take part in the discussion.
   a) I was prepared for it.
   b) It was too deep for me.
   c) I had to take sides.

IV. Is it true or false?

	T	F
1. Books have pages.	☐	☐
2. Prisoners are free men.	☐	☐
3. Popular books sell well.	☐	☐
4. Poor people have lots of money.	☐	☐
5. Poison is dangerous.	☐	☐

	T	F
6. "Prince" is a title.	☐	☐
7. Pigeons have wings.	☐	☐
8. Pale colours are bright.	☐	☐
9. Patient people always complain.	☐	☐
10. Farmers plough their fields.	☐	☐
11. A pair is a fruit.	☐	☐
12. Libraries are quiet places.	☐	☐
13. People take pride in their failures.	☐	☐
14. Painters raise pigs and grow wheat.	☐	☐

Have you plenty of spare *time?* Then take *a sheet of paper* and *put down as many pairs* of words *as possible* which, in English, are *pronounced* the same but are spelt differently. We'll start you off: "*pair*" and "*pear*".

V. Find the nouns which go together.

A. 1. priest, 2. politics, 3. patient, 4. potato, 5. prisoner, 6. pond, 7. queen, 8. passenger, 9. pass

a) prison, b) church, c) water, d) flight, e) mountain, f) king, g) hospital, h) vegetable, i) party

B. 10. prince, 11. poet, 12. picture, 13. performance, 14. pardon, 15. payment, 16. plough, 17. pear, 18. prayer

j) frame, k) farmer, l) bill, m) fruit, n) kingdom, o) mercy, p) poem, q) play, r) religion

C. 19. plant, 20. pigeon, 21. page, 22. pack, 23. pig, 24. powder, 25. photograph, 26. pot

s) pan, t) book, u) flower, v) dust, w) bird, x) film, y) ham, z) cards

Now watch the new words which you've learned *pile up!*

VI. Find the words which go together.

A. 1. to win .... 2. to serve ..... 3. to raise ..... 4. to turn ..... 5. to make .....

a) the page, b) preparations, c) a prize, d) a question, e) the purpose

B. 6. to own ..... 7. to solve ..... 8. to take ..... 9. to read ..... 10. to wrap ..... 11. to keep .....

f) a passage, g) a picture, h) a problem, i) property, j) a promise, k) a parcel

C. 12. to plant ..... 13. to park ..... 14. to play ..... 15. to pull ..... 16. to polish .....

l) a tooth, m) a car, n) crops, o) cards, p) your shoes

D. 17. to provide ..... 18. to put ..... 19. to protect .....

q) from, r) for, s) off

E. 20. to quiet ..... 21. to pass ..... 22. to pick .....

t) out, u) away, v) down

VII. Put in the right noun.

1. Today's game was called off because several ..... were hurt during the practice yesterday afternoon.
2. "I have almost finished this book. I have only a few ..... left to read!"
3. In the desert, oil is pumped through ..... for great distances.
4. The first ..... on the debt is due on 15th August.
5. An economical housewife compares ..... when she goes shopping.
6. "Shall I make a ..... of tea, or would you prefer to have coffee?"
7. A narrow ..... leads up the side of the hill to our cottage.
8. The ..... is the king's wife.
9. Many nervous people have high blood .....
10. When people go camping, they carry their supplies in a light ..... on their backs.
11. Because she was still under age, Helen could not accept Edward's marriage ..... until she had received her parents' .....
12. "Would you care for another ..... of cake?"
13. One of the most serious ..... which faces man today is the growth of the world population.
14. It is not known exactly when the ..... was painted.
15. I had forgotten my gloves, so I put my hands in my coat ..... to keep them warm.
16. A .....'s job is to make sure that people obey the law.
17. Sudden ..... in the chest are often a sign of heart disease.
18. According to the weather report, there is a ..... of rain this afternoon.
19. ..... is change which brings improvement.
20. The angry ..... between the boys quickly developed into a fight.

21. People usually use thin ..... for air-mail letters.
22. The American puts "gas" in his car, but the Englishman asks for .....
23. ..... have been trained to carry messages between places which are over a thousand miles from each other!
24. When the old man died, his few ..... were given to his nephew.
25. Man normally seeks pleasure and avoids .....
26. "I simply can't agree with your ..... of view."
27. The rich always have ..... to eat; the poor seldom have enough.
28. The various parts of a city are often called ".....". Paris, for instance, is famous for its student ....., which lies on the left bank of the Seine.
29. Both ..... and ministers are religious leaders.
30. Munich, Oslo, Paris and Amsterdam are all pleasant ..... to visit in the spring.
31. Everything is taking shape according to .....!
32. "All ..... travelling to Madrid must change trains at Marseilles."
33. When people work fast, they sometimes sacrifice quality for .....
34. The driver who wins the race will receive first .....
35. Taking a walk with a friend, reading a good book, travelling, listening to music—these are just a few of life's .....!
36. A popular type of ..... consists of hundreds of small pieces. When these pieces are put together properly, they form a .....
37. The ....., one of the most common vegetables in the world, can be prepared in many different ways.
38. I'm certain that his letter was in that ..... of papers on my desk, but at the moment I can't find it!
39. The ..... of the bill was to provide new job opportunities for unemployed people.
40. Each of the political ..... in a country represents a different point of view on matters of national interest.
41. If you cannot read small ....., then perhaps you need glasses.
42. There were no tickets available for the evening ..... of the play.
43. Ships from all over the world are loaded and unloaded every day in Rotterdam, which is one of Europe's largest .....
44. Before a man begins to build a house, he must first draw up a .....
45. The roots, leaves and berries of many wild ..... can be eaten.
46. One of the most serious problems in world politics is that rich, powerful nations are often in a good ..... to control the futures of the poorer, developing countries.
47. When everyone was seated, the minister began the service by reading two ..... from the Bible.
48. Carl Sandburg, T. S. Eliot and Robert Frost are three famous twentieth century American .....

49. Despite the ..... of hundreds of policemen, large crowds gathered in the streets to protest against the goverment's new defence plans.

Although the various *peoples of the world* speak different native tongues, many also know a foreign language. English, *in particular*, is *quite popular*. Whenever you travel, "*pack*" it with the rest of your "*provisions*"*!*

VIII. Put in the right verb.

1. Farmers ..... their fields before they plant their crops.
2. "Would you please ..... me another cup of coffee?"
3. We were not ..... to enter the factory until we had shown our passes.
4. The sign at the entrance to the park said: "Keep off the grass and don't ..... the flowers!"
5. It's a good idea always to ..... your bills on time.
6. Children like to ..... at being "grown-up".
7. In some countries murder is ..... with death.
8. Just laws ..... the rights of all citizens.
9. The first books were ..... in Germany in about 1450.
10. Many English words, such as "poor" and "pour", are ..... in the same way, but are written differently.
11. Do you know how to ..... any foreign dishes?
12. Every week my mother ..... the furniture to make it shine.
13. Unless a large number of citizens ..... against the new tax bill, it will soon become law.
14. If you intend to play an instrument well, you must ..... every day!
15. It's an ancient custom for children to ..... eggs bright colours at Easter time.
16. When Doctor Brown retired, the members of his staff ..... him with a small gift.
17. In most societies it is the man who ..... food and shelter for the family.
18. The flowers which we ..... in our garden early in the spring bloomed all summer.
19. Before the student answered the question, he ..... for a moment to think.
20. "I can't ..... you that I'll be there, but I'll try to come!"
21. The police ..... the young man at length about his activities on the night of the murder.
22. Modern medicine can ..... man from many serious diseases which used to kill thousands of people.

23. It's so difficult to find a place to ..... the car that I seldom drive into the city.
24. We ..... the glasses carefully in a large, heavy box before we shipped them abroad.
25. A wise man learns how to ..... from his mistakes.
26. I tried to ..... him to continue his education, but he refused to listen to reason.
27. Although British and American citizens ..... many words differently, as a rule they can understand one another with little difficulty.

IX. Put in the right adjective.

1. It's safe to drink ..... water.
2. During elections, tax reform often becomes an important ..... issue.
3. ..... officers fight crime.
4. "Have you a ..... colour in mind, madam, or will any of these towels do?"
5. Anyone may swim in a ..... swimming pool.
6. That's certainly a ..... lamp. I've never seen one quite like it before!
7. On Sunday we spent a ..... day by the sea, just swimming, playing ball and lying in the sun.
8. A ..... wound hurts.
9. Patience, confidence, pride and courage are valuable ..... qualities which everyone should try to acquire.
10. Many people are ..... against certain groups of people because of their race or religion.
11. The public seldom learns the results of ..... talks between world leaders.
12. It's possible, but not very ....., that you'll ever catch a fish with your bare hands!
13. Having worked hard for many years in order to become a successful farmer, my father has good reason to feel ..... of his farm, home and family.
14. Cats are very ..... animals. When they hunt for birds or mice they often lie in the grass for a long time without making a sound.
15. My niece looked very ..... in her new dress!
16. Do you realize that some modern weapons are ..... enough to destroy whole cities in minutes?
17. Twenty years ago few people thought that it would ever be ..... for man to fly to the moon!
18. Because he was not afraid to question the truth of certain beliefs and ideas, Socrates was not ..... with his fellow citizens.

X. Put in the right word.

(It doesn't always begin with the letter 'P' or 'Q'. Be careful!)

1. Although my brother is a doctor ..... profession, he's also a well-known painter.
2. While I was in France, I paid a ..... to my relatives there.
3. You're wasting your time if you attend school but don't pay .....
4. Factory workers must learn to put ..... with a lot of noise.
5. "I have a lot of ideas, but I never have time to put them ..... on paper!"
6. If a person refuses to pay taxes, the government will ..... possession of his property.
7. If everything goes ..... to plan, we should be in Madrid by Sunday.
8. During the spring fair, which always ..... place in the town park, a number of groups ..... native dances and sing until midnight every night.
9. "Let me just put ..... my hat and coat, and then I'll be ready to go!"
10. In many parts of the world, cotton is still planted and ..... by hand.
11. When my mother goes shopping, she tries to pick ..... only fresh fruit and vegetables.
12. If you drive carefully, you can usually prevent an accident ..... happening.
13. When I was a boy, I loved to play ..... on my sisters!
14. Because we worked quickly, we were able to put ..... the fire before there was any serious damage.
15. I will be able to pay ..... all the money I've borrowed as soon as I find a job.
16. If her young are threatened, a mother bear will try to protect them ..... harm.
17. "What's the matter with John? He ..... past me and didn't even speak!"
18. In his paper the student presented only those facts which supported his point of .....
19. Although you may first apply for a job by post, you will almost always have to present yourself ..... person later.
20. "Never put ..... until tomorrow something which you can do today!"
21. The mechanic couldn't repair my car right away because he had no ..... parts on hand.
22. At the last stop, all the remaining ..... got off the bus.
23. Work on the new town-hall is currently ..... progress; as yet, however, only a few rooms are completely finished.

24. "I can recommend Mr Williams. He is a person who takes great ..... in his work.
25. As the man already spent forty per ..... of his wages on rent, he couldn't afford to move to a larger house.
26. A large number of farmers and workers support the party which is now ..... power.
27. Representatives of the firm met ..... private to discuss the plans for extending the factory.

That's quite enough! Now check your answers. *Are you pleased with* your *progress?* One hundred *per cent* right is "*perfect*". But don't *go to pieces* if you made a few mistakes—*there's no point in that!*

Key

I 1b, 2b, 3a, 4b, 5a, 6c, 7b, 8c, 9a, 10c, 11b, 12a, 13b, 14c, 15b, 16c

II 1b, 2a, 3a, 4c, 5b, 6a, 7b, 8c, 9a, 10c, 11b, 12c, 13b, 14a, 15c, 16c, 17b, 18a, 19c, 20b, 21b, 22b, 23c, 24a, 25b, 26a

III 1b, 2a, 3b, 4c, 5b, 6a, 7c, 8a, 9b, 10b, 11b, 12a, 13a, 14c, 15b

IV 1T, 2F, 3T, 4F, 5T, 6T, 7T, 8F, 9F, 10T, 11F, 12T, 13F, 14F

V A. 1b, 2i, 3g, 4h, 5a, 6c, 7f, 8d, 9e, — B. 10n, 11p, 12j, 13q, 14o, 15l, 16k, 17m, 18r — C. 19u, 20w, 21t, 22z, 23y, 24v, 25x, 26s

VI A. 1c, 2e, 3d, 4a, 5b — B. 6i, 7h, 8g, 9f, 10k, 11j — C. 12n, 13m, 14o, 15l, 16p — D. 17r, 18s, 19q — E. 20v, 21u, 22t

VII 1 players, 2 pages, 3 pipes, 4 payment, 5 prices, 6 pot, 7 path, 8 queen, 9 pressure, 10 pack, 11 proposal, permission, 12 piece, 13 problems, 14 picture, 15 pockets, 16 policeman, 17 pains, 18 possibility, 19 progress, 20 quarrel, 21 paper, 22 petrol, 23 pigeons, 24 possessions, 25 pain, 26 point, 27 plenty, 28 quarters, quarter, 29 priests, 30 places, 31 plan, 32 passengers, 33 quantity, 34 prize, 35 pleasures, 36 puzzle, picture, 37 potato, 38 pile, 39 purpose, 40 parties, 41 print, 42 performance, 43 ports, 44 plan, 45 plants, 46 position, 47 passages, 48 poets, 49 presence

VIII 1 plough, 2 pour, 3 permitted, 4 pick, 5 pay, 6 play, 7 punished, 8 protect, 9 printed, 10 pronounced, 11 prepare, 12 polishes, 13 protest, 14 practise, 15 paint, 16 presented, 17 provides, 18 planted, 19 paused, 20 promise, 21 questioned, 22 protect, 23 park, 24 packed, 25 profit, 26 persuade, 27 pronounce

IX 1 pure, 2 political, 3 police, 4 particular, 5 public, 6 peculiar, 7 pleasant, 8 painful, 9 personal, 10 prejudiced, 11 private, 12 probable, 13 proud, 14 patient, 15 pretty, 16 powerful, 17 possible, 18 popular

X 1 by, 2 visit, 3 attention, 4 up, 5 down, 6 take, 7 according, 8 takes, perform, 9 on, 10 picked, 11 out, 12 from, 13 tricks, 14 out, 15 back, 16 from, 17 walked/went, 18 view, 19 in, 20 off, 21 spare, 22 passengers, 23 in, 24 pride, 25 cent, 26 in, 27 in

How many mistakes have you made?

	I to VI	VII to IX	X	
Excellent	0—12	0—11	0— 2	mistakes
Good	13—24	12—22	3— 5	mistakes
Satisfactory	25—37	23—33	6— 8	mistakes
Not very good	38—60	34—47	9—13	mistakes
Weak	over 60	over 47	over 13	mistakes

R for Radio

What can you *hear on the radio? All the year round* you can listen to *a wide range* of music, including your favourite *records*. You can also *receive* special *reports* of car *races* and other sports events. The news and weather *reports* are broadcast *regularly* too. After an election, the *results* are always *announced over the radio*. You can even hear a *religious* service! *Rush* over to your *radio* and turn it on *right now!*

I. What's the opposite?

1. I never *received* the card which you
   a) sent from Zurich.
   b) wrote in Zurich.
   c) left in Zurich.

2. When prices were *reduced*, sales
   a) increased.
   b) fell.
   c) stopped.

3. *Don't rush!*
   a) Hurry up!
   b) Take your time!
   c) Keep still!

4. Dry skin feels *rough*, not
   a) smooth.
   b) stiff.
   c) soft.

5. I *remembered* to buy bread, but I
   a) intended to buy eggs!
   b) refused to buy eggs!
   c) forgot to buy eggs!

6. "Turn *right* at this corner, then turn
   a) left."
   b) around."
   c) north."

7. "*Right now* I'm busy. I'll call you back
   a) again!"
   b) soon!"
   c) later!"

8. Do *the rich* understand the problems of
   a) the young?
   b) the poor?
   c) the workers?

9. Our cat *ran away* one day, and never
   a) returned!
   b) escaped!
   c) turned up!

10. Ten answers were *right*. Only one was
    a) satisfactory.
    b) perfect.
    c) wrong.

11. If you *rent* a house, you don't
   a) hire it.
   b) own it.
   c) seize it.

12. The sun *rises* in the morning and
   a) settles in the evening.
   b) sets in the evening.
   c) sits in the evening.

Don't stop now! *You have the right of way!*

II. Which word or phrase has almost the same meaning?

1. *That's really too much!*
   a) That's a shame!
   b) That's going too far!
   c) That's hardly enough!

2. *The curtain will rise at eight.*
   a) The show will end at eight.
   b) The show will begin at eight.
   c) The show lasts until eight.

3. *Give me a ring* next week!
   a) give me a call
   b) marry me
   c) ask me

4. Crops are usually planted *in rows.*
   a) in large fields
   b) in straight lines
   c) in good soil

5. My friend Tom *runs* a machine in a large factory.
   a) repairs
   b) produces
   c) operates

6. Will you *remain* abroad much longer?
   a) stay
   b) study
   c) struggle

7. His *remarks* were to the point.
   a) conditions
   b) complaints
   c) comments

8. *First-rate* films are
   a) valuable
   b) famous
   c) excellent

9. *Nothing else remains to be done!*
   a) We've almost finished!
   b) We've finished!
   c) We haven't finished!

10. When does the train *reach* Lisbon?
   a) set out for
   b) arrive in
   c) leave from

11. Who *is responsible for* these mistakes?
    a) made
    b) noticed
    c) corrected

12. *As a rule* I don't like lazy people.
    a) to tell the truth
    b) in a nutshell
    c) generally

13. "Did you *really* say that?"
    a) actually
    b) accidentally
    c) actively

14. *At any rate*, we had better leave soon!
    a) in short
    b) under these circumstances
    c) in any case

You can't *get rid of* us yet. We never *run out* of new words!

III. Which choice makes sense?

1. Remember me to your father!
    a) He doesn't know me!
    b) I haven't seen him for years!
    c) I've forgotten what he looks like!

2. "Can you reach that pan?
    a) I don't need it!"
    b) I wash my hands of it!"
    c) I can't get at it!"

3. "Road under repair!
    a) Drive slowly!"
    b) Speed up!"
    c) Go ahead!"

4. There was no more room on the train.
    a) All the seats were reserved.
    b) It was completely empty.
    c) We easily found a seat.

5. Will you please repeat that?
    a) It's a waste of time!
    b) I couldn't hear you!
    c) That goes without saying!

6. Our television needs to be repaired.
    a) The programmes are awful.
    b) It's in good condition.
    c) It doesn't work.

7. Please turn off the radio!
    a) I can't hear it!
    b) It's disturbing me!
    c) That's my favourite song!

8. A person driving on the main road has the right of way
    a) if he has a map.
    b) when there is no other traffic.
    c) at road junctions.

9. It's raining hard outside!
   a) Let's take a walk!
   b) Open the window!
   c) Where's my umbrella?

Don't be a poor sport. *You have no right to hold us responsible for* your mistakes!

IV. Is it true or false?

	T	F
1. Houses have roofs.	☐	☐
2. Lions roar.	☐	☐
3. A rose is a fruit.	☐	☐
4. Rope is stronger than string.	☐	☐
5. A race is a sports event.	☐	☐
6. You'll be ill if you eat ripe fruit!	☐	☐
7. The sun rises in the evening.	☐	☐
8. Blood is red.	☐	☐
9. A king is a ruler.	☐	☐
10. Rocks float.	☐	☐
11. It's faster to walk than to run.	☐	☐
12. A ready-made suit is made to order.	☐	☐
13. You shouldn't refuse a reasonable offer!	☐	☐
14. Ruins are modern buildings.	☐	☐
15. There's no traffic during the rush hour.	☐	☐

May we make a *recommendation?* It will be easier for you to *remember* difficult words and expressions if you *repeat* the exercises from time to time!

V. Find the nouns which go together.

A. 1. roast
2. rest
3. right
4. rain
5. record
6. relation
7. rail
8. ruler

a) wrong, b) drop, c) uncle, d) train, e) beef, f) leader, g) music, h) sleep

B. 9. religion
10. roof
11. ring
12. right
13. representative
14. radio
15. rose
16. roll

i) finger, j) house, k) government, l) flower, m) belief, n) bread, o) broadcast, p) left

C. 17. rope
18. relatives
19. red
20. rank
21. remedy
22. road
23. root

q) colour, r) medicine, s) tree, t) junction, u) knot, v) captain, w) family

VI. Find the words which go together.

A. 1. to read .....
2. to ring ....
3. to risk .....
4. to raise .....
5. to ride .....
6. to run .....

a) a business, b) taxes, c) a bicycle, d) a bell, e) a book, f) one's life

B. 7. to round off .....
8. to reserve ....
9. to rule out .....
10. to run .....
11. to reply to.....

g) a possibility, h) a letter, i) a corner, j) a seat, k) a machine

C. 12. to listen to .....
13. to win .....
14. to break .....
15. to have .....

l) a race, m) the right of way, n) the radio, o) a rule

D. 16. to break .....
17. to take .....
18. to make .....
19. to pay .....
20. to let .....

p) rooms, q) the rent, r) a record, s) a request, t) a rest

If you *had regrets* about the last exercises, don't *hand in your resignation* yet. *In the long run* everything will *turn out all right!*

VII. Put in the right noun.

1. A bank must keep an exact ..... of every account.
2. Leaves and ..... are important parts of plants.
3. Army officers are distinguished by .....
4. I wrote to him several months ago, but I've never received a .....
5. When my father became manager of the store, he received a ..... in pay.
6. Young girls often wear ..... in their hair.
7. Breakfast in many European countries consists of ....., butter, jam and a cup of coffee.
8. Since the road we usually take was under ....., we had to go home a different way.
9. The car was travelling at the ..... of 90 miles per hour when the accident happened.
10. When you apply for a job, it's helpful to have favourable letters of .....

11. Although the play received bad ..... from the critics, I enjoyed it very much.
12. A world sports ..... is rarely broken.
13. The best ..... for a cold is to get plenty of .....!
14. The Nile, the Amazon and the Mississippi are the three longest ..... in the world.
15. A game is played according to a set of .....
16. My collection of ..... includes both popular and serious music.
17. The experiments of Georg Ohm led to the discovery of electrical .....
18. The band's performance was perfect in every .....!

VIII. Put in the right verb.

1. Policemen ..... their own lives in order to save the lives of other people.
2. "Did you ever ..... the message which I left with your secretary?"
3. Two men with guns ..... the bank just before it closed.
4. Have you ever ..... a horse?
5. When my father reaches the age of sixty-five, he intends to .....
6. Please ..... two seats for me for Friday night's performance.
7. A country's leaders ..... its people abroad.
8. A quick and convenient way to add up figures is first to ..... them off.
9. In small towns throughout Europe you can hear the church bells ..... on Sunday mornings.
10. When I returned to the town where I was born, it had changed so much that I hardly ..... it!
11. During the game, the ball ..... out of the yard and into the street.
12. You should ..... the tires on your car when they become worn out.
13. I highly ..... that you visit Heidelberg. It is full of interesting sights.
14. A person never ..... how difficult it is to raise a family until he has one.
15. "I called in order to ..... you of the meeting this afternoon. Don't forget to tell William about it, too!"
16. When I was a child, my mother used to ..... aloud to me every night until I fell asleep.
17. During the recent elections, three men ..... for the office of President.
18. John ..... that he hadn't finished school. He couldn't find a job anywhere.

19. It is difficult to ..... ink stains from clothing.
20. When we heard that my aunt had become very ill, we ..... to the hospital to see her.
21. You bake bread, but you ..... beef!
22. Yesterday on the train I ..... across an old friend with whom I went to school!
23. During his speech, the company representative ..... to the recent electrical workers' strike.
24. When I had my tooth pulled, the doctor gave me some medicine to ..... the pain.
25. The customs officials ..... us to open our luggage before we could cross the border.

It really isn't very far to the end now—but don't try to set a *speed record!*

IX. Put in the right adjective or adverb.

1. Apples and pears taste best when they're .....
2. Circles are perfectly .....
3. Everyone was very ..... to hear that the little boy had been found.
4. In the spring, shops sell their winter clothes at ..... prices.
5. "You are ....., I was wrong!"
6. Animals eat their food ....., but man usually cooks his food before he eats it.
7. "Be .....! Try to consider my point of view as well as your own!"
8. Certain ..... ideas, such as God, heaven, the devil and hell have influenced the behaviour of people for centuries.
9. I would ..... go to the cinema tonight than stay at home.
10. Some animals which were common twenty years ago are quite ..... today.

X. Put in the right word.

(It doesn't always begin with 'R'. Be careful!)

1. "Are you ready ..... the next question?"
2. These cars are on sale at reduced prices because we must ..... room for next year's models.
3. "Watch out! That bicycle has the right of .....!"
4. Did you hear the news ..... the radio this morning?
5. The police haven't ruled ..... the possibility of murder in this case.
6. To what extent should parents be ..... responsible for the actions of their children?

7. "When you see Robert, ... him my best regards!"
8. What's a good remedy ..... a splitting headache?
9. During the rush ..... the streets are crowded with cars, buses, trams, people and bicycles!
10. As we drove along the country road we saw fields of tall, ripe corn ..... our right and left.
11. ..... a result of the operation, my brother is able to walk again.
12. "Everything will ..... out all right. Don't worry."
13. When I reached ..... the glass of milk, I knocked it over.
14. This city reminds me very much ..... Paris.
15. "Things are going from bad to worse. ..... are rising, and hundreds of people are unemployed."
16. Nowadays young people can choose from a ..... range of occupations.
17. ..... what reason have you decided to change jobs?
18. "..... many respects the plan is a good one, but it will not solve all our problems."
19. No matter how much medicine I take, I can't ..... rid of this cold!
20. The prisoner was freed ..... the request of the king.
21. When I made those remarks, I was speaking ..... the record, and not as a representative of the company."
22. "Perhaps the book will sell well, and perhaps it won't. That remains to be .....!"
23. "..... to reason. He'll stop at nothing. You don't stand a chance!"
24. "Tell him to call me right ..... It's urgent!"
25. Careless driving is the cause of most road .....
26. We ran ..... of petrol on the way home.
27. The sun shines here all the ..... round!

You can *take a rest! Nothing else remains to be done!*

Key

I 1a, 2a, 3b, 4a, 5c, 6a, 7c, 8b, 9a, 10c, 11b, 12b

II 1b, 2b, 3a, 4b, 5c, 6a, 7c, 8c, 9b, 10b, 11a, 12c, 13a, 14c

III 1b, 2c, 3a, 4a, 5b, 6c, 7b, 8c, 9c

IV 1T, 2T, 3F, 4T, 5T, 6F, 7F, 8T, 9T, 10F, 11F, 12F, 13T 14F, 15F

V A. 1e, 2h, 3a, 4b, 5g, 6c, 7d, 8f — B. 9m, 10j, 11i, 12p, 13k, 14o, 15l, 16n — C. 17u, 18w, 19q, 20v, 21r, 22t, 23s

VI A. 1e, 2d, 3f, 4b, 5c, 6a — B. 7i, 8j, 9g, 10k, 11h — C. 12n, 13l, 14o, 15m — D. 16r, 17t, 18s, 19q, 20p

VII 1 record, 2 roots, 3 rank, 4 reply, 5 raise, 6 ribbons, 7 rolls, 8 repair, 9 rate, 10 recommendation, 11 reviews, 12 record, 13 remedy, rest, 14 rivers, 15 rules, 16 records, 17 resistance, 18 respect

VIII 1 risk, 2 receive, 3 robbed, 4 ridden, 5 retire, 6 reserve, 7 represent, 8 round, 9 ring/ringing, 10 recognized, 11 rolled, 12 replace, 13 recommend, 14 realizes, 15 remind, 16 read, 17 ran, 18 regretted, 19 remove, 20 rushed, 21 roast, 22 ran, 23 referred, 24 relieve, 25 required/requested

IX 1 ripe, 2 round, 3 relieved, 4 reduced, 5 right, 6 raw, 7 reasonable, 8 religious, 9 rather, 10 rare

X 1 for, 2 make, 3 way, 4 on, 5 out, 6 held, 7 give, 8 for, 9 hour, 10 to/on, 11 as, 12 turn, 13 for, 14 of, 15 prices, 16 wide, 17 for, 18 in, 19 get, 20 at, 21 off, 22 seen, 23 listen, 24 away, 25 accidents, 26 out, 27 year

How many mistakes have you made?

	I to VI	VII to IX	X	
Excellent	0—10	0— 5	0— 2	mistakes
Good	11—20	6—10	3— 5	mistakes
Satisfactory	21—31	11—15	6— 8	mistakes
Not very good	32—47	16—27	9—13	mistakes
Weak	over 47	over 27	over 13	mistakes

S for Smile

Let's suppose that you're a *stranger* in a country where everyone *speaks* English. You may feel that *you don't stand a chance*. But *that doesn't make any sense* at all. Just *smile* and *speak up!* You'll be *surprised* to *see* what happens. New friends, a good meal, a cup of coffee or tea—*all sorts of things* are *in store for you.*

I. What's the opposite?

1. My *son* is ten; my
   a) niece is twelve.
   b) daughter is twelve.
   c) cousin is twelve.

2. People who *seldom* sleep well
   a) often feel tired.
   b) never feel tired.
   c) sometimes feel tired.

3. The River Rhine flows from *south* to
   a) west.
   b) north.
   c) east.

4. Don't *speed up* before a dangerous curve!
   a) Yield!
   b) Stop!
   c) Slow down!

5. I *sold* my old bicycle and
   a) ordered a new one.
   b) bought a new one.
   c) fetched a new one.

6. *Sour* cherries aren't
   a) sweet!
   b) sweat!
   c) sweep!

7. How do you distinguish between *success* and
   a) curiosity?
   b) ability?
   c) failure?

8. *Pride* is the opposite of
   a) sorrow.
   b) shame.
   c) silence.

9. If you worry a lot, *small* problems will become
   a) funny ones.
   b) simple ones.
   c) big ones.

10. My *sister* likes to read; my
    a) nephew likes to write.
    b) brother likes to swim.
    c) father likes to paint.

11. I *sent* him a letter, but I haven't
    a) received a reply yet.
    b) posted a reply yet.
    c) asked for a reply yet.

12. Do you usually walk *slowly* or
    a) quickly?
    b) quietly?
    c) softly?

13. The young man *stood up* so that the old woman could
    a) settle down.
    b) sit down.
    c) slow down.

14. *Second-hand* books cost less than
    a) used ones.
    b) new ones.
    c) good ones.

15. *Single* men aren't
    a) healthy.
    b) married.
    c) faithful.

16. I could *start* the machine but I couldn't
    a) repair it!
    b) operate it!
    c) stop it!

17. Two houses may look the *same* from the outside but be quite
    a) different inside.
    b) cheerful inside.
    c) alike inside.

You can *set a good example* to your friends if you *start* to *speak* English a little bit *after school* or after work. It's easy to *say such* things as "Good-bye," "*Dinner is served*," "*Sorry*," and "*So long!*"

II. Which word or phrase has almost the same meaning?

1. This bowl is a *splendid* example of early Chinese art!
   a) ancient
   b) poor
   c) fine

2. I'm *sure* that he'll come soon.
   a) afraid
   b) certain
   c) determined

3. "*Please take a seat!*"
   a) "Please remove that chair!"
   b) "Please sit down!"
   c) "Please make room for me!"

4. Cortez sailed to America *in search of* gold.
   a) to look for
   b) to ask for
   c) to catch sight of

5. German beer is *second to none!*	a) all the same! b) second-rate! c) the very best!
6. *Suddenly* it started to rain.	a) before long b) all at once c) at last
7. We *went to see* our relatives last week-end.	a) wrote to b) visited c) telephoned
8. "That's not a *simple* question!"	a) easy b) serious c) reasonable
9. I feel *somewhat* tired tonight.	a) extremely b) unusually c) a bit
10. Production was *stepped up* to meet demand.	a) held up b) kept up c) increased
11. "*I'm on his side!*"	a) "I agree with him!" b) "I'm against him!" c) "I like him!"
12. On Christmas day we were all *in good spirits!*	a) busy b) happy c) religious
13. *Does this colour suit your taste?*	a) Do you like it? b) Does it taste good? c) Does it fit?
14. "Dinner will be ready *soon!*"	a) first of all b) in good time c) before long
15. You *seem to be* angry about something.	a) appear to be b) refuse to be b) expect to be
16. "*I see!*"	a) "I know!" b) "I remember!" c) "I understand!"
17. *It's safe to say* that Mr Thompson will win the election.	a) there's no chance b) there's no doubt c) there's no possibility

18. Early in the morning we *set out for* the mountains.
    a) found out about
    b) started out for
    c) came down from

19. "*The date completely slipped my mind!*
    a) I never knew about it!"
    b) I meant to ask about it!"
    c) I forgot about it!"

20. *All sorts of* books were for sale.
    a) a number of
    b) many second-hand
    c) all kinds of

21. Thomas is *set on becoming* a doctor.
    a) sure to become
    b) determined to become
    c) about to become

22. "*It's a shame* you can't come to the party!"
    a) I'm sorry that
    b) I'm glad that
    c) I'm angry that

Can you spare a minute? We have a *suggestion* or two. First of all, don't work too long *at a stretch*—a *solid* hour of *steady* work each day *should serve* you well. *Secondly, there's not the slightest hurry. Make sure* that you *study* each exercise carefully!

III. Which choice makes sense?

1. "Keep a stiff upper lip—
    a) don't show your feelings!"
    b) you'll make it!"
    c) shut up!"

2. It's a secret.
    a) Don't tell anyone.
    b) Everyone knows!
    c) I heard it on the radio.

3. Make it short!
    a) We haven't much time!
    b) It's too long now!
    c) There's no rush.

4. If you run short of money,
    a) you can pay me back.
    b) you can borrow some from me.
    c) you can go into business.

5. He was all smiles
    a) after he had lost the money.
    b) after he had won the race.
    c) after he had had the accident.

6. Can you spare a minute?
    a) I need some help.
    b) My watch is broken.
    c) Leave me alone!

7. "Don't be in such a hurry!
   a) You'll never get anywhere!"
   b) There's plenty of time!"
   c) Come on, let's go!"

8. We cut our trip short
   a) because we enjoyed it so much.
   b) because the children became ill.
   c) because the weather was perfect.

9. "Speak up!
   a) Don't sit down!"
   b) You're shouting!"
   c) I can't hear you!"

10. "Shut the window!
    a) It's warm outside!"
    b) It's cold in here!"
    c) It's a beautiful day!"

11. Stand up for your rights!
    a) Don't let other people take advantage of you.
    b) Don't let other people advise you.
    c) Don't let other people argue with you.

12. I was so worried
    a) that I didn't sleep a wink all night.
    b) that I slept like a top!
    c) that I fell asleep right away.

13. That doesn't make sense to me.
    a) I see what you mean.
    b) Please explain it again.
    c) I get it!

14. See me tomorrow.
    a) I have some spare time now.
    b) I've nothing to do at the moment.
    c) I'm awfully busy today.

15. The factory shut down
    a) in order to increase production.
    b) because business was good.
    c) during the strike.

16. John was kept in after school
    a) because he had done his homework.
    b) because he was late in the morning.
    c) because he got good marks.

17. By a stroke of luck,
    a) I won the match!
    b) I lost the game!
    c) I dropped the ball!

18. In the summer
    a) I usually wear a fur coat.
    b) I often go for a swim.
    c) I frequently play in the snow.

19. We stayed with relatives
    a) while we were at home.
    b) while we were on holiday.
    c) while we were on our own.

20. People who work in the same office
   a) like to talk shop.
   b) always go shopping together.
   c) draw the same salary.

21. Since he was about to give up his job,
   a) he settled down to work.
   b) he went on strike.
   c) he let things slide.

22. The flight leaves at eight o'clock sharp.
   a) It may leave later!
   b) Don't be late!
   c) It's never on time!

23. Why don't you stay at home tomorrow
   a) if you feel better?
   b) if you feel well?
   c) if you feel ill?

24. I couldn't see over the wall.
   a) It was too low!
   b) It was too thick!
   c) It was too high!

It's safe to say that you will have to *spend* more time on this lesson than on the others. *Since* "S" is a "big" letter, everything here is *on a large scale!* But there's no need *to be in low spirits—at this stage* in your *studies* you're *scarcely starting from scratch. Settle down to work*—"*full steam ahead!*"

IV. Is it true or false?

		T	F
1.	Beer is a soft drink.	☐	☐
2.	Silk comes from sheep.	☐	☐
3.	Silver is a metal.	☐	☐
4.	Stiff materials bend easily.	☐	☐
5.	A slave is a free man.	☐	☐
6.	You can see a shadow.	☐	☐
7.	Sailors work on ships.	☐	☐
8.	Stupid people learn quickly.	☐	☐
9.	You can touch silence.	☐	☐
10.	Common sense is nonsense.	☐	☐
11.	A swallow is a snake.	☐	☐
12.	Supper is served in the morning.	☐	☐
13.	Europe is south of Africa.	☐	☐
14.	Some parents spoil their children.	☐	☐
15.	Salary is a vegetable.	☐	☐
16.	You can smell smoke.	☐	☐
17.	Successful businessmen are poor.	☐	☐
18.	Sugar is sour.	☐	☐
19.	Good scissors cut well.	☐	☐

	T	F
20. A saw is a fruit.	☐	☐
21. Monkeys swing from trees.	☐	☐
22. Modest people like to show off.	☐	☐
23. Steel is a gas.	☐	☐
24. Steam is a solid.	☐	☐
25. You have one shoulder.	☐	☐
26. The sun is smaller than the earth.	☐	☐
27. Swords are dangerous weapons.	☐	☐
28. There's always a lot of traffic in dead-end streets.	☐	☐
29. You can find shells on the sea shore.	☐	☐

Just imagine! Each new word is a *source* of new ideas and thoughts. Pause for a moment. Think about the ideas which *surround* the words "*stranger*", "*sea*", "*soul*", and "*struggle*", for instance. Doesn't each of these words *suggest* to you a whole "world" of experience?

V. Find the nouns which go together.

A. 1. stamp 2. silver 3. stock 4. shower 5. sister 6. shoes 7. screen 8. soup

a) brother, b) rain, c) store, d) stockings, e) bowl, f) gold, g) letter, h) cinema

B. 9. suit 10. son 11. snow 12. smoke 13. scene 14. story 15. soldier 16. supper

i) writer, j) army, k) play, l) clothes, m) meal, n) winter, o) chimney, p) daughter

C. 17. season 18. steel 19. screw 20. stage 21. second 22. storm 23. sound 24. shoe

q) nut, r) echo, s) thunder, t) spring, u) iron, v) foot, w) theatre, x) minute

Don't leave a single stone unturned! New words are *springing up like mushrooms!*

VI. Find the words which go together.

A. 1. to keep .... 3. to hear ...... 5. to collect .....
2. to express ..... 4. to go for ..... 6. to put on .....

a) a swim, b) your shoes, c) stamps, d) a sound, e) a secret, f) sympathy

B. 7. to wear ..... 9. to draw..... 11. to sing .....
8. to climb ..... 10. to take ..... 12 to tell .....

g) a song, h) a story, i) a suit, j) stairs, k) a salary, l) a seat

C. 13. to set .... 15. to spend ..... 17. to sweep .....
14. to smoke ..... 16. to stir ...... 18. to steer .....

m) a car, n) the floor, o) time, p) an example, q) a pipe, r) tea

D. 19. to shake ..... 21. to serve ..... 23. to saddle .....
20. to sew on ..... 22. to say .....

s) a horse, t) good-bye, u) dinner, v) hands, w) a button

In the exercises which follow, *all sorts of surprises* are *in store for* you. We can *swear to that!*

VII. Put in the right noun.

1. Winter is the coldest ..... of the year.
2. It's very difficult to remove oil ..... from clothes.
3. We began the evening meal with a bowl of hot vegetable .....
4. ..... is a fine cloth which is produced on a large scale in Japan and China.
5. "Is there a pair of ..... anywhere in the house? I want to cut a picture out of the newspaper!"
6. ..... is an especially hard and strong metal.
7. Have you ever tried to count the stars in the ..... at night?
8. After such a long ..... of fine weather, we're certain to have some rain before long!
9. "Don't forget to put a ..... on that letter before you post it!"
10. The ..... of a river is often a spring or a small mountain stream.
11. The ..... beside the gate said: "Private property. Keep out."
12. Once a week my wife puts clean ..... on all the beds in the house.
13. My grandmother never went to ..... She taught herself to read and write.
14. Before an important election, a great deal of political activity takes place behind the .....

15. At a clearance ..... you can buy all kinds of things at reduced prices!
16. Autumn follows ....., and ..... follows winter.
17. ..... answer the telephone, type letters, prepare reports and do other office work.
18. Water covers roughly seventy per cent of the world's .....
19. ..... provide protection for many sea animals; hens' eggs also have hard .....!
20. In a theatre the action takes place on the .....
21. We climbed ten flights of ..... before we reached the top floor of the office building.
22. After the party last night, ... took my coat by mistake!
23. In the bank, money and valuable papers are kept in a .....
24. My favourite record is ruined! There's a deep ..... on one side of it!
25. At the cinema films are shown on a .....
26. "I'll tell you a ..... if you promise not to tell anyone else!"
27. Each of the four roses was a different ..... of red.
28. India, which was a British colony for nearly two hundred years, became an independent ..... in 1947.
29. At present there are twenty doctors on the hospital .....
30. While I was waiting at the bus ....., I read the evening newspaper.
31. The express train from Dover arrived at Victoria ..... in London five minutes early.
32. The water in rivers and lakes is fresh, but sea water contains .....
33. We were so pleased with the ..... at the small restaurant that we left the waiter a large tip!
34. Have you any brothers and .....?
35. Most people need from seven to eight hours ..... every night.
36. Many animals which can't see well depend largely on their sense of ..... in order to find food and avoid danger.
37. In *The Iliad* Homer tells the ..... of the Trojan War.
38. The ..... provides the earth with heat and light.
39. During my short ..... in Paris I visited Notre Dame, the Eiffel Tower and the Louvre.
40. During the past year, the city has taken several ..... to improve traffic conditions in the city centre.
41. That ..... of road which winds through the mountains is extremely dangerous.
42. The water wasn't deep, so I took off my .... and ..... and walked across the small mountain stream.
43. As we walked along the ....., we picked up small stones and shells and put them in our pockets.

44. These gloves don't fit me. They're the wrong .....
45. I always become nervous when I have to make a ..... in front of a large group of people.
46. The ..... on the top of many high mountains never melts, even during the summer.
47. The farmer returned from the market with two heavy ..... of potatoes.
48. When a person rides a horse, he sits in the .....
49. Loud ..... can damage a person's ears.
50. After a week had passed, the police called off the ..... for the missing boys.
51. When Mr Johnson died, each of his three sons received an equal ..... of the family property.
52. Once the traffic had stopped, the blind man's dog led him across the .....
53. I tied the old letters together with a piece of .....
54. "Listen! He's singing one of my favourite .....!"
55. Yesterday the President made an official ..... to the press about his recent trip abroad.

Did you just escape by the skin of your teeth? We're not *surprised!* After all, those *sentences* certainly weren't *simple.*

VIII. Put in the right verb.

1. Although the problem looked easy, it took me two hours to .... it!
2. I ..... the medicine as fast as I could. It tasted terrible!
3. The young man quickly ..... the horse, then jumped on and rode away.
4. Before we left the party we ..... good-bye to all the other guests.
5. "You had better not play with the cat's tail, Steve. He'll ..... you!"
6. The young man was so nervous that his hand ..... as he reached for the cup of coffee.
7. There are better ways to ..... a quarrel than to fight!
8. Last winter our neighbour ..... on the ice and broke his arm.
9. The telephone connection between London and Paris was so bad that I had to ..... before my brother could hear me.
10. Can you ..... any foreign languages besides English?
11. A high stone wall completely ..... the old castle.
12. No wonder your car won't ..... There's no petrol in it!
13. While we were in Stockholm, we ..... with friends because hotels were so expensive.

14. I told my friend to ..... away from the old well in the field behind our house, but he wouldn't listen to me.
15. Monkeys use their long arms and tails to ..... from tree to tree.
16. A woman who knows how to ..... can make many of her own clothes.
17. When a boy begins to grow a beard, he must learn how to .... !
18. On a clear day on the plains you can ..... for miles in every direction.
19. Police ..... the house from top to bottom, but they couldn't find any trace of the stolen money.
20. It's not lawful for hunters to ..... certain wild animals for sport.
21. After supper we sat around the camp fire and ..... songs.
22. As the girl threw the coin into the water and watched it ..... to the bottom, she crossed her fingers and wished for good luck.
23. Which countries ..... the world with most of its oil?
24. The policeman jumped into the icy river in order to ..... the boy's life.
25. The young man appeared to be very nervous. As he told me about his troubles, he ..... one cigarette after another.
26. When my brother and I tried to saw the board in half, it ..... into several pieces.
27. At the end of the term a number of students decided to ..... the play which they had written in class.
28. How long does it take for a ship to ..... from Europe to America?
29. Nowadays many farmers use machines to ..... the cream from the milk.
30. Since the young man who sat beside me on the train looked hungry, I ..... my lunch with him.
31. People from almost every country of the world have ..... in America during the last three hundred years.
32. When I'm in London I always go to ..... my aunt who lives there.
33. "Come on, let's go! I can't wait to ..... you the new bicycle I got for Christmas!"
34. The organ doesn't ..... at all out of tune to me, even though no one has played it for several years.
35. My aunt frequently ..... from such severe headaches that she has to stay in bed all day.
36. Even though Thomas has two jobs, he still can't make enough money to ..... his wife and six children.
37. Every few hours the bus stopped so that the passengers could get out, walk around a bit and ..... their arms and legs.
38. "But I'm telling the truth! I'll ..... to it in court!"
39. Some people never learn how to ..... because they are afraid of water.

40. Since there weren't enough seats in the hall for everyone, quite a few people had to .....
41. The thieves ..... two valuable paintings from the art collection.
42. During the quarrel one man ..... the other by the arm and threatened to hit him!
43. When the wind blows, it often ..... the seeds of plants and flowers for miles in every direction.
44. A person shouldn't ..... more money than he earns!
45. When a man works hard on a hot day and ..... a lot, his body loses a great deal of salt.
46. The beauty of the park was ..... by all the papers, bottles and cans which people had left behind them.
47. As children, we loved to ..... down the hill behind our house when it was covered with snow.
48. When nobody was looking, the bank clerk ..... his lunch bag full of money!
49. University students have to ..... for weeks to prepare for their examinations.

We have a *secret* to *share* with you. *From start to finish we've been on your side! Isn't that a stroke of luck?*

IX. Put in the right adjective or adverb.

1. Milk which is not fresh tastes .....
2. Your homework is perfect. You haven't made a ..... mistake!
3. Are you absolutely ..... that this information is correct?
4. I left the office in ..... a hurry that I forgot to lock the safe!
5. ..... people like to live in a rented flat; others prefer to own their own home.
6. The instructions were so ..... that anyone could understand them!
7. In English, both personal and business letters often end with, "Yours ....."
8. It isn't easy for a ..... person to make new friends.
9. In many large cities today it isn't ..... for a person to walk alone in the streets at night.
10. "Don't mix these two shades of blue paint together—keep them .....!"
11. Egg shells feel ..... and hard, not rough and .....
12. Do you think that ..... in space there exist other living beings?
13. I don't understand what you're laughing about. This is a very ..... matter!
14. ..... I like being with friends, at other times I need to be alone.
15. Although he's so old, my grandfather is ..... in body and mind.

16. Some insects are so ..... that you can hardly see them.
17. A ..... businessman is one who makes a lot of money!
18. Some religious groups live according to very ..... rules of behaviour.
19. People put sugar in their tea to make it taste .....
20. Our dog is so ..... that he can't do even the simplest tricks!
21. Many people never move; they live in the ..... house all their lives.
22. When a person is asleep or resting his heart beats more ..... than when he is active.
23. All the leaves have fallen from the trees, and it is much colder. Winter will ..... be here.
24. As the snow began to fall, it became so ..... in the forest that we could hear the slightest sound.
25. Brazil is the largest country in ..... America.
26. ..... I'll manage to pay this month's rent, even though I haven't enough money at the moment.
27. We can't use that ladder! It's too ..... to reach the windows on the fourth floor.
28. Young children like books with short, ... words and lots of pictures.
29. The road stretches ..... across the desert for hundreds of miles.
30. "In my opinion," the judge told the court, "death is too ..... a punishment for this man's crime."
31. Tools, metal containers and other objects which have ..... edges should be kept out of the reach of children.
32. The four sides of a square are all the ..... length!

Slow down—the end is *in sight!*

X. Put in the right word.

(It doesn't always begin with 'S'. Be careful!)

1. When the factory was shut ...., many men lost their jobs.
2. The directions on the bottle said, "Shake well ..... using!"
3. "Don't be late! The train leaves ..... ten o'clock sharp!"
4. "Where is the town-hall?" "It's straight ..... You can't miss it!"
5. In autumn many small animals store ..... large supplies of seeds, nuts and other food for the winter.
6. The book was so interesting that I stayed ..... all night in order to finish it.
7. I've read this poem over and over again, but it still doesn't ..... sense to me!"
8. Since English is not his strong ....., Robert will probably fail the test.

9. Why are so many houses in this neighbourhood ..... sale?
10. As the plans for our trip began to ..... shape, I became more and more excited.
11. "It's a ..... that you can't stay longer. The party is just getting under way!"
12. "Miss Smith, will you please ..... to it that these letters are typed before you leave this evening?"
13. "..... ! I didn't mean to push you!"
14. The cold weather didn't really set ..... until December this year.
15. I would like to help you out, but I ..... no say in the matter.
16. "That serves him ..... ! He never cared about anyone but himself anyway!"
17. Tickets for the concert were sold ..... a month in advance, so we couldn't get any.
18. I was so worried about the accident that I didn't sleep a ..... all night.
19. John had changed so much that at ..... sight I didn't even recognize him!
20. I've been studying English so much that I'm sick ..... it!
21. We set ..... for Marseilles, but we only got as far as Paris!
22. "Well, ... of the sort happened while I was there."
23. ..... of a sudden the wind changed direction, the sky became dark and it began to pour with rain.
24. The instructions were quite difficult to understand. I had to read them several ..... before I was able to set ..... work.
25. "I'm in a hurry so ..... it short!"
26. Even though he can't afford it, John is set ..... buying a new car.
27. This book has always sold ..... It's a favourite with people of all ages.
28. During the struggle one man was shot ....., and two police officers were seriously wounded.
29. I refused to ..... sides in the quarrel. It was none of my business.
30. "Don't forget to switch ..... the light in the sitting-room before you go to bed."
31. My friend and I always stick ..... no matter what happens!
32. We stayed ..... London for a week; then we spent a few days in the country.
33. He's my best friend. He stood ..... me even when I was in trouble.
34. When my sister left for the university, the whole family saw her ..... at the station.
35. Our relatives who live in the country were snowed ..... quite often this winter.
36. In many countries people shake ..... when they meet one another.

37. You don't stand a ..... of getting a job. You haven't enough experience.
38. "Are you ..... my side or hers? Make up your mind!"
39. His feelings of jealousy spring ..... a lack of confidence in himself.
40. On ..... ship we spent the days watching the ocean, swimming in the pool and playing cards.
41. "What a stroke of .....! We've won a free trip to London!"
42. Can you name a man who has.....great service to your country?
43. The sudden attack ..... the soldiers by surprise.
44. This year when we cleaned the cellar, we threw out all sorts ..... things which we didn't need any more.
45. A sailor needs only a few personal possessions while he's ..... sea.
46. "I know that it isn't your job, but do it ..... my sake!"
47. According to the weather report, there's bad weather in store ..... us this week-end.
48. Barbara has given me the ..... shoulder all week, ever since we had that quarrel on Saturday night.
49. "Stand up ..... your rights! Don't let him take advantage of you!"
50. Are there usually large numbers of poor people in a country which has a high standard of .....?
51. We ..... sight of the ship within a few minutes after it left the harbour.

Check your answers. If *you are satisfied* with the results, you *should be all smiles* now!

Key

I 1b, 2a, 3b, 4c, 5b, 6a, 7c, 8b, 9c, 10b, 11a, 12a, 13b, 14b, 15b, 16c, 17a

II 1c, 2b, 3b, 4a, 5c, 6b, 7b, 8a, 9c, 10c, 11a, 12b, 13a, 14c, 15a, 16c, 17b, 18b, 19c, 20c, 21b, 22a

III 1a, 2a, 3a, 4b, 5b, 6a, 7b, 8b, 9c, 10b, 11a, 12a, 13b, 14c, 15c, 16b, 17a, 18b, 19b, 20a, 21c, 22b, 23c, 24c

IV 1F, 2F, 3T, 4F, 5F, 6T, 7T, 8F, 9F, 10F, 11F, 12F, 13F, 14T, 15F, 16T, 17F, 18F, 19T, 20F, 21T, 22F, 23F, 24F, 25F, 26F, 27T, 28F, 29T

V A. 1g, 2f, 3c, 4b, 5a, 6d, 7h, 8e — B. 9l, 10p, 11n, 12o, 13k, 14i, 15j, 16m — C. 17t, 18u, 19q, 20w, 21x, 22s, 23r, 24v

VI A. 1e, 2f, 3d, 4a, 5c, 6b — B. 7i, 8j, 9k, 10l, 11g, 12h — C. 13p, 14q, 15o, 16r, 17n, 18m — D. 19v, 20w, 21u, 22t, 23s

VII 1 season, 2 stains, 3 soup, 4 silk, 5 scissors, 6 steel, 7 sky, 8 spell, 9 stamp, 10 source, 11 sign, 12 sheets, 13 school, 14 scenes, 15 sale,

16 summer, spring, 17 secretaries, 18 surface, 19 shells, shells, 20 stage, 21 stairs, 22 someone/somebody, 23 safe, 24 scratch, 25 screen, 26 secret, 27 shade, 28 state, 29 staff, 30 stop, 31 Station, 32 salt, 33 service, 34 sisters, 35 sleep, 36 smell, 37 story, 38 sun, 39 stay, 40 steps, 41 stretch, 42 socks, shoes, 43 shore, 44 size, 45 speech, 46 snow, 47 sacks, 48 saddle, 49 sounds, 50 search, 51 share, 52 street, 53 string, 54 songs, 55 statement

VIII 1 solve, 2 swallowed, 3 saddled, 4 said, 5 scratch, 6 shook, 7 settle, 8 slipped, 9 shout, 10 speak, 11 surrounds/surrounded, 12 start, 13 stayed, 14 stay, 15 swing, 16 sew, 17 shave, 18 see, 19 searched, 20 shoot, 21 sang, 22 sink, 23 supply, 24 save, 25 smoked, 26 split, 27 stage, 28 sail, 29 separate, 30 shared, 31 settled, 32 see, 33 show, 34 sound, 35 suffers, 36 support, 37 stretch, 38 swear, 39 swim, 40 stand, 41 stole, 42 seized, 43 scatters, 44 spend, 45 sweats, 46 spoiled/spoilt, 47 slide, 48 stuffed, 49 study

IX 1 sour, 2 single, 3 sure, 4 such, 5 some, 6 simple, 7 sincerely, 8 shy, 9 safe, 10 separate, 11 smooth, soft, 12 somewhere, 13 serious, 14 sometimes, 15 sound, 16 small, 17 successful, 18 strict, 19 sweet, 20 stupid, 21 same, 22 slowly, 23 soon, 24 still, 25 South, 26 somehow, 27 short, 28 simple, 29 straight, 30 severe, 31 sharp, 32 same

X 1 down, 2 before, 3 at, 4 ahead, 5 up, 6 up, 7 make, 8 point, 9 for, 10 take, 11 shame, 18 see, 13 sorry, 14 in, 15 have, 16 right, 17 out, 18 wink, 19 first, 20 of, 21 out, 22 nothing, 23 all, 24 times, to 25 make, 26 on, 27 well, 28 dead, 29 take, 30 off, 31 together, 32 in, 33 by, 34 off, 35 in, 36 hands, 37 chance, 38 on, 39 from, 40 board, 41 luck, 42 done/rendered, 43 took, 44 of, 45 at, 46 for, 47 for, 48 cold, 49 for, 50 living, 51 lost

How many mistakes have you made?

	I to VI	VII to IX	X	
Excellent	0—14	0—17	0— 5	mistakes
Good	15—28	18—34	6—10	mistakes
Satisfactory	29—43	35—51	11—15	mistakes
Not very good	44—70	52—68	16—25	mistakes
Weak	over 70	over 68	over 25	mistakes

T for Touch

Language is one of the *tools* of *thought*—with it we can *translate* our feelings into words. "*How are things?*" ... "When do you want *to get together?*" ... "We *had a good time* last night!" ... "Let's *keep in touch!*"

I. What's the opposite?

1. He *lost his temper*, but I
   a) became excited
   b) kept my head
   c) kept it in my mind
2. *Tame* animals are no longer
   a) wild.
   b) weak.
   c) wise.
3. *Tight* knots hold better than
   a) thick ones.
   b) loose ones.
   c) strong ones.
4. *Tender* meat is not
   a) lean.
   b) tough.
   c) raw.
5. When I travel I *take along* a few essentials and
   a) leave everything else behind.
   b) put off everything else.
   c) forget about everything else.
6. Mrs Miller is *tall* and *thin*, but her husband is
   a) long and thin!
   b) high and heavy!
   c) short and fat!
7. Nobody ever stops *learning*, even those who
   a) teach.
   b) try.
   c) test.
8. *These* stamps are American;
   a) yours are British.
   b) those are British.
   c) they are British.
9. I *told* you *the truth*. I didn't
   a) laugh about it.
   b) lie about it.
   c) learn about it.
10. In exercise IV you must decide what is *true* or
    a) false.
    b) opposite.
    c) correct.
11. How many people *take* more than they
    a) admit?
    b) need?
    c) give?

12. Four applications were *turned down* and only one was
   a) acquired.
   b) accepted.
   c) accounted for.

13. I *turned off* the radio and
   a) turned on the television.
   b) turned down the television.
   c) turned up the television.

14. A *single ticket* costs less than a
   a) double ticket.
   b) return ticket.
   c) second-hand ticket.

15. Don't *throw out* those old books. I want to
   a) sell them!
   b) keep them!
   c) read them!

16. I *took off* my work clothes and
   a) got out a suit and tie.
   b) put on a suit and tie.
   c) took down a suit and tie.

Let's *come to terms!* We'll "*trade*" you new words for your work!

II. Which word or phrase has almost the same meaning?

1. *How tall are you?*
   a) What's your weight?
   b) What's your height?
   c) What's your size?

2. We *had a good time* in Paris.
   a) enjoyed ourselves
   b) behaved ourselves
   c) astonished ourselves

3. Babies have *tender* skin.
   a) pale and thin
   b) nice and healthy
   c) soft and delicate

4. *I slept like a top.*
   a) I slept very well.
   b) I couldn't fall asleep.
   c) I didn't sleep a wink.

5. *What's the trouble?*
   a) What's the news?
   b) What's the matter?
   c) What's the use?

6. *These days* most families have a telephone.
   a) nowadays
   b) up to now
   c) from now on

7. We will be finished *in no time!*
   a) once and for all
   b) very soon
   c) in the long run

8. It's never a pleasant *task* to clean the cellar!	a) job b) event c) feeling
9. Last week I had a *terrible* cough.	a) slight b) awful c) mild
10. *It's your turn!*	a) You're next! b) Watch out! c) Turn over!
11. The history *test* was easy!	a) lesson b) examination c) question
12. *All told* there were a hundred pictures on display.	a) all joking aside b) generally speaking c) altogether
13. We cleaned the house *from top to bottom.*	a) thoroughly b) bit by bit c) from time to time
14. Have you ever *travelled* abroad?	a) walked b) been on a trip c) sailed
15. May I come *too?*	a) also b) anyhow c) again
16. *To date* I have completed a year of study.	a) for the time being b) just now c) up to now
17. We couldn't *come to terms on* the proposal.	a) delay b) agree on c) act on
18. I *talk over* my problems with my brother.	a) discuss b) solve c) overcome
19. *At times* I have pains in my chest.	a) at the moment b) every day c) now and then
20. I hope that you will *think over* what I have said.	a) consider b) support c) believe

If you meet someone who speaks English, *keep in touch with him! Get together from time to time. To your surprise,* you may soon be able *to talk together* for hours!

III. Which choice makes sense?

1. Turn on the light!
   a) I want to go to sleep!
   b) It's too dark in here!
   c) It's too bright in here!

2. Why should I take the blame?
   a) I'm guilty!
   b) It was my idea!
   c) It's not my fault!

3. The game ended in a tie.
   a) Neither team won.
   b) Our team won.
   c) It was called off.

4. It's in bad taste
   a) to arrive on time.
   b) to make fun of someone.
   c) to set a good example.

5. The judge cleared his throat;
   a) then he began to speak.
   b) then he took a nap.
   c) then he listened to reason.

6. I tore up the note and
   a) threw it away.
   b) kept it.
   c) posted it.

7. When the temperature is low,
   a) it's cold.
   b) the sky is clear.
   c) it usually rains.

8. Try on this coat.
   a) It's too short for you.
   b) It should fit you.
   c) It's not your size.

9. Everything will turn out all right.
   a) It's merely a matter of time.
   b) I'm really worried.
   c) The situation is hopeless.

10. My sister has a sweet tooth.
    a) She's a sweet person.
    b) She has a bad tooth.
    c) She loves sweets.

11. I'm sorry, but my hands are tied.
    a) I won't help you out.
    b) I can't help you out.
    c) I'll never help you out.

12. This won't do.
    a) It isn't good enough.
    b) It's just right.
    c) It's perfect!

13. Joe and I are on bad terms.
    a) He broke his word to me.
    b) He's my best friend.
    c) We are badly paid.

14. Please turn down the television.
    a) It's too soft.
    b) I am trying to study.
    c) I want to watch it.

15. All the seats on the bus were taken,
    a) so I sat down.
    b) so I stood.
    c) so I took turns.

16. I am tired of hearing about it.
    a) Tell me again!
    b) Let's drop the subject!
    c) Don't forget to remind me!

17. For the time being,
    a) you can live here.
    b) it's three o'clock.
    c) tell the truth.

18. It's nothing to speak of.
    a) Don't tell anybody!
    b) Don't worry about it!
    c) It's very important!

19. I tried to get in touch with you last night,
    a) but there was no answer.
    b) but you were at home.
    c) but you answered the telephone.

20. John takes after his father.
    a) They both have a lot of common sense.
    b) They're not a bit alike.
    c) They go everywhere together.

IV. Is it true or false?

	T	F
1. Dogs wag their tails.	☐	☐
2. A good band plays out of tune.	☐	☐
3. You should never trust a thief!	☐	☐
4. A century is a thousand years.	☐	☐
5. You can touch a thought.	☐	☐
6. A saw is a tool.	☐	☐
7. Trees have leaves.	☐	☐
8. Treasures are worthless.	☐	☐
9. It's easy to trick a fool.	☐	☐
10. A towel is a curtain.	☐	☐
11. You can sleep in a tent.	☐	☐

	T	F
12. Most books have a table of contents.	☐	☐
13. Tomorrow is already here.	☐	☐
14. A thirsty man needs water.	☐	☐
15. Your teeth are in your mouth.	☐	☐
16. A tribe is larger than a family.	☐	☐

Are you still *in a good temper? Then hold on tight*—the next exercises may *give you some trouble!*

V. Find the nouns which go together.

A. 1. tail
2. time
3. thread
4. thirst
5. table
6. title
7. tea
8. toe
9. tune

a) needle, b) chair, c) book, d) leaf, e) dog, f) foot, g) song, h) water, i) clock

B. 10. tip
11. theatre
12. tailor
13. tears
14. toy
15. ticket
16. type
17. test
18. tree

j) doll, k) clothes, l) play, m) sort, n) branch, o) money, p) mark, q) train, r) eyes

C. 19. tie
20. term
21. trousers
22. tool
23. trial
24. tin
25. tobacco
26. thunder

s) pipe, t) storm, u) court, v) metal, w) shirt, x) school, y) hammer, z) belt

VI. Find the words which go together.

A. 1. to drink .....
2. to have .....
3. to pay .....
4. to watch .....
5. to learn .....
6. to clear .....
7. to lose .....
8. to have .....

a) television, b) taxes, c) a trade, d) a sweet tooth, e) tea, f) your throat, g) a good time, h) your temper

B. 9. to get .....
10. to tell .....
11. to take.....
12. to hold .....
13. to be .....
14. to go .....
15. to keep.....

i) in touch, j) the trouble, k) in trouble, l) by tram, m) tight, n) a walk, o) the truth

C. 16. to try ..... 18. to trade .....
17. to tear ..... 19. to talk .....

p) up, q) over, r) on, s) in

What are you thinking about at the moment? Nothing to speak of? Then just for the fun of it, *try* the next exercises. *How about that?*

VII. Put in the right noun.

1. ..... is a popular British drink.
2. We usually refer to a book by its .....
3. The thieves disappeared without leaving a .....
4. Cigarettes are made from .....
5. Young children play with .....
6. Should you always leave a waiter a ..... ?
7. When you walk, your ..... help you to keep your balance.
8. The school year is divided into three .....
9. Since I don't like driving, I always travel by .....
10. Yesterday was Friday; ..... is Saturday; ..... will be Sunday!
11. Have you a needle and ..... so that I can sew on this button?
12. In the desert people live in .....
13. Angry people have a ..... to become violent.
14. If you want to get in touch with someone quickly, send him a .....
15. Mr White is a mechanic by .....
16. For a small boy it's a difficult ..... to go shopping!
17. In the winter you can often see animal ..... in the snow.
18. My father lost his ..... during the quarrel.
19. I couldn't call you because our ..... was out of order.
20. Between the ages of six and twelve, most children lose their first set of ..... and acquire a second set.
21. ..... take place in court.
22. Never sign an agreement unless you understand all the .....!
23. A person who has a ..... is ill.
24. ..... work with needle and thread.
25. I was in such a rush this morning that I only had ..... for a cup of coffee!
26. When a young man first enters the army, he receives several months of .....
27. You talk and taste with your .....
28. You can find out the age of a tree from the number of rings in its .....
29. When you write a paper, make certain that you leave plenty of space at the ..... and bottom of each page.

Do you feel tired out? Take our advice: don't work *too long* at a stretch. *Every now and then take a walk, get together* with a friend or even *take a nap. Trust us! We're telling the truth!*

VIII. Put in the right verb

1. It often ..... during a storm.
2. Never ..... your old clothes—they might come into fashion again!
3. An efficient secretary can ..... over seventy words per minute.
4. Can you ..... these sentences into your native tongue?
5. Since there was only one brush, we had to ..... turns at painting.
6. Some dogs can be ..... to lead blind people.
7. On the radio you can ..... in to broadcasts from all over the world.
8. "This milk ..... sour."
9. "How can I open this bottle?" "Just ..... off the cap!"
10. Most instruments must be ..... up before they are played.
11. In Germany many families ..... a walk on Sunday afternoons.
12. "Guess who ..... up at the party last night—my old girl friend!"
13. In the fifth century B. C. (before Christ), Herodotus ..... widely throughout Europe and Asia.
14. A good hunter can ..... an animal through the forest without making any noise.
15. "If I were you, I wouldn't ..... him—he may not be telling the truth!"
16. We ..... in our old car for a new one.
17. "Please can you tell me the way to the station?" "..... left at the next corner, then go straight ahead."
18. "If you don't at least ....., you'll never get anywhere."
19. I ..... off the corner of a piece of paper and wrote down his address and telephone number.

Are we still *on good terms* after *those* last "*terrible*" sentences? *We're sorry about that,* but we're determined to *teach* you English *from top to bottom!*

IX. Put in the right adjective or adverb.

1. It takes ..... as long to drive from Frankfurt to Hamburg as it does from Munich to Nuremberg.
2. "I'm .....! May I have a glass of water?"
3. "Did the train arrive .....?" "No, it was ten minutes late."
4. My old trousers don't fit any more. They're too .....!
5. A ..... animal is not afraid of people.

6. Although I worked late last night, I don't feel at all ..... this morning.
7. Paul and Joan spend all their time ..... They're very much in love.
8. If the present rate of growth continues, the ..... population of the world will double by the year 2000.
9. As a tree grows, it becomes .....
10. The weather was ..... while we were on holiday. It rained every day.

X. Put in the right word.

(It doesn't always begin with 'T'. Be careful!)

1. "I don't want that ..... sugar. I only want a little.
2. "Take off those dirty shoes this ..... before you ruin the carpet!"
3. I have to wear glasses ..... the time. Otherwise I can't see a thing!
4. Charles is ..... trouble because he cheated in the examination.
5. In many countries there is a high tax ..... cigarettes and petrol.
6. Mary's eyes ..... with tears as she read the telegram from home.
7. "You're very quiet. What are you thinking .....?"
8. The two nations ..... to terms on a new defence agreement.
9. "What are they talking .....?" "I don't know. It's too deep for me!"
10. Our next door neighbours ..... us a lot of trouble. They ought to mind their own business!
11. During the war the army took ..... all the schools and other public buildings.
12. I tore the advertisement ..... of the newspaper and saved it.
13. "..... are things?" "Fine, thanks."
14. I made up my mind then ..... there to put my foot down!
15. "I don't ..... a thing about it. I wasn't in yesterday."
16. ..... though I was angry, I tried to be polite.
17. The poet ..... his throat and then began to read aloud.
18. He'll find out about it sooner or later. It's merely a ..... of time.
19. How do you manage to read and watch television at the ..... time?
20. "I wouldn't treat this matter ..... You're in serious trouble."
21. The car turned the corner at top ..... and went straight into a tree.
22. It's almost impossible to translate a poem ..... another language.
23. "We have one ..... of trousers in your size, but they're rather expensive."
24. Some of the instruments were ..... of tune. The band sounded terrible!

25. "Turn the bottle of orange juice upside ..... and shake it well before you open it."
26. My father always ..... his temper when he discusses politics.
27. "You had better take ..... that remark about my father. It's not true."
28. To his mother's surprise, Robert took a frog ..... of his pocket!
29. When I fell off my bicycle, I tore a ..... in my trousers.
30. "Take my ..... Don't drive in the city during the rush hour!"
31. I took ..... his name and address for future reference.
32. "Thank you very ..... for your help."
33. "This door is locked. ..... about that one?"
34. "It doesn't matter if it snows later this evening. ..... then we'll be home."
35. My father traded ..... his old TV when he bought a new one.
36. "Let's try to ..... in touch with each other from now on!"
37. "The path ends here. We'll have to turn ....."
38. "You were right—it's no use." "I told you .....!"
39. When my girl friend lost weight, she had to take ..... all her dresses.
40. John was completely ..... in thought. He didn't even hear us come into the room!
41. When the meeting was called off, no one even ..... the trouble to give me a ring.

Key

I 1b, 2a, 3b, 4b, 5a, 6c, 7a, 8b, 9b, 10a, 11c, 12b, 13a, 14b, 15b, 16b,

II 1b, 2a, 3c, 4a, 5b, 6a, 7b, 8a, 9b, 10a, 11b, 12c, 13a, 14b, 15a, 16c, 17b, 18a, 19c, 20a

III 1b, 2c, 3a, 4b, 5a, 6a, 7a, 8b, 9a, 10c, 11b, 12a, 13a, 14b, 15b, 16b, 17a, 18b, 19a, 20a

IV 1T, 2F, 3T, 4F, 5F, 6T, 7T, 8F, 9T, 10F, 11T, 12T, 13F, 14T, 15T, 16T

V A. 1e, 2i, 3a, 4h, 5b, 6c, 7d, 8f, 9g — B. 10o, 11l, 12k, 13r, 14j, 15q, 16m, 17p, 18n — C. 19w, 20x, 21z, 22y, 23u, 24v, 25s, 26t

VI A. 1e, 2d/g, 3b, 4a, 5c, 6f, 7h, 8g/d — B. 9i, 10o, 11jn, 12m, 13k, 14l, 15i — C. 16r, 17p, 18s, 19q

VII 1 tea, 2 title, 3 trace, 4 tobacco, 5 toys, 6 tip, 7 toes, 8 terms, 9 train, 10 today/tomorrow, 11 thread, 12 tents, 13 tendency, 14 telegram, 15 trade, 16 task, 17 tracks, 18 temper, 19 telephone, 20 teeth, 21 trials, 22 terms, 23 temperature, 24 tailors, 25 time, 26 training, 27 tongue, 28 trunk, 29 top

VIII 1 thunders, 2 throw away, 3 type, 4 translate, 5 take, 6 trained, 7 tune, 8 tastes, 9 twist, 10 tuned, 11 take, 12 turned, 13 travelled, 14 track, 15 trust, 16 traded, 17 turn, 18 try, 19 tore

IX 1 twice, 2 thirsty, 3 on time, 4 tight, 5 tame, 6 tired, 7 together, 8 total, 9 taller, 10 terrible

X 1 much, 2 minute, 3 all, 4 in, 5 on, 6 filled, 7 about, 8 came, 9 about, 10 give, 11 over, 12 out, 13 how, 14 and, 15 know, 16 even, 17 cleared, 18 matter, 19 same, 20 lightly, 21 speed, 22 into, 23 pair, 24 out, 25 down, 26 loses, 27 back, 28 out, 29 hole, 30 advice, 31 down, 32 much, 33 how, 34 by, 35 in, 36 keep, 37 back, 38 so, 39 in, 40 lost, 41 took

How many mistakes have you made?

	I to VI	VII to IX	X	
Excellent	0—12	0— 6	0— 4	mistakes
Good	13—24	7—12	5— 8	mistakes
Satisfactory	25—36	13—18	9—12	mistakes
Not very good	37—60	19—30	13—20	mistakes
Weak	over 60	over 30	over 20	mistakes

U and V for Unusual View

"*As I understand it ...*" Words are *useful* when they help *us* to *understand* another's *views*. For example, you may *attach great value* to certain things and ideas which don't seem *valuable* to other people. *Under these circumstances*, you must choose your words carefully, or no one else will *understand* what you really think and feel. Is this an *unusual view* of the *value* of language?

I. What's the opposite?

1. A painting may seem *ugly* to me but
   a) natural to you.
   b) simple to you.
   c) beautiful to you.
2. *Victory* means success;
   a) progress means failure.
   b) application means failure.
   c) defeat means failure.
3. Our cat couldn't get *under* the fence, so she jumped
   a) over it.
   b) through it.
   c) into it.
4. We climbed *up* one side of the mountain and
   a) above the other.
   b) across the other.
   c) down the other.
5. Pots and pans are *useful* to a cook, but
   a) usual to a tailor.
   b) useless to a tailor.
   c) unknown to a tailor.
6. A person may be *unable* to speak a foreign language, yet be
   a) able to read it.
   b) anxious to read it.
   c) afraid to read it.
7. At home the bedrooms and bathroom are *upstairs*, and all the other rooms are
   a) out of doors.
   b) downstairs.
   c) inside.

II. Which word or phrase has almost the same meaning?

1. *What's up?*
   a) Who are you?
   b) What's the matter?
   c) How do you do?
2. City property is *valuable*.
   a) cheap
   b) expensive
   c) worthless

3. *Up to now* it's been cold for spring.
   a) until now
   b) in the future
   c) sooner or later

4. Our grocer carries *a large variety of* fresh vegetables.
   a) a small number of
   b) a few kinds of
   c) all sorts of

5. It's *up to you* to take care of your own personal affairs.
   a) none of your business
   b) beyond your power
   c) your concern

Up to now we have helped you with many difficult words. Soon, however, *it will* all *be up to you!*

III. Which choice makes sense?

1. He isn't up yet.
   a) He's brushing his teeth.
   b) He's still asleep.
   c) He's tied down.

2. Your time is up.
   a) It's my turn now.
   b) Keep on working.
   c) I must wind my watch.

3. What's the use of trying?
   a) We have nothing to lose.
   b) We have everything to gain.
   c) We don't stand a chance.

4. He's hard up for money now
   a) because he's supposed to be rich.
   b) because business is good.
   c) because he's lost his job.

IV. Is it true or false?

	T	F
1. Roses are vegetables.	☐	☐
2. Villages are large cities.	☐	☐
3. Honesty is a virtue.	☐	☐
4. Your vote expresses your choice.	☐	☐
5. Valuable papers should be kept under lock and key.	☐	☐
6. Unions protect the workers' interests.	☐	☐
7. Your uncle is your father's brother.	☐	☐
8. Urgent matters must be attended to immediately.	☐	☐
9. It's unusual to carry an umbrella in the rain.	☐	☐
10. Unemployed people have jobs.	☐	☐
11. Famous artists are unknown.	☐	☐
12. An unfavourable review praises a writer's work.	☐	☐

Try to *use up* all the following words!

V. Find the nouns which go together.

1. voice
2. umbrella
3. union
4. vote
5. verse
6. university
7. vegetable
8. uncle
9. victory

a) aunt, b) poem, c) battle, d) student, e) potato, f) rain, g) song, h) election, i) worker

VI. Find the words which go together.

1. to pay .....
2. to vote ....
3. to use ....
4. to attach.....

a) force, b) value to, c) a visit, d) down

Don't forget that it's *useless* just to know the meanings of new words. You need to know how to *use* each word properly, too!

VII. Put in the right noun.

1. If it's raining, take an .....!
2. A singer must study for years before she develops full control of her .....
3. In 1492 Columbus set out on a long and dangerous ..... to the New World.
4. Long poems consist of many .....
5. From the top of the mountain we looked down to the valley below, and saw the small ..... where we spent the night.
6. Some of Germany's finest wines come from the ..... of the River Moselle.
7. In ..... of your good references, we'll give you the job, although you lack the necessary experience.
8. Many kinds of fruit and ..... are good for you.
9. In some parts of the world, women wear ..... over their faces whenever they appear in public.
10. A serious student makes full ..... of all material available to him.
11. Many prisoners' sentences were reduced by ..... of their good behaviour.
12. Freedom is of little ..... without justice.

VIII. Put in the right verb.

1. The situation is so serious that I ..... you to act immediately.
2. Although I arrived in New York a month ago, I still can't get ..... to the noise and traffic.

3. Among other things, you can ..... a knife to cut bread and prepare vegetables.
4. Do you think man will ..... up all the world's raw materials within a century?
5. Last year, when my brother was in hospital with a broken leg, I ..... him every day.
6. The people of the town ..... down the plans for a new town-hall.
7. It needed a strong leader to ..... the divided country.
8. I ..... to work at night. Now, I can't get ..... to working during the day!
9. You will ..... another person better if you speak his language.
10. At large European ports, many ships are loaded and ..... daily.

What's the use of stopping now? *Victory* is just around the corner!

IX. Put in the right adjective or preposition.

1. When a baby is ....., he cries.
2. I can stay ..... tomorrow; then I must return home.
3. A ..... person thinks mostly about his appearance.
4. In some countries it's ..... that a man's children will take care of him when he grows old.
5. Because the road was ..... repair, we had to slow down and drive carefully.
6. ..... men use force.
7. ..... storms can cause great damage.
8. In spite of last night's severe snow storm, schools will be open today as .....

X. Put in the right word.

(It doesn't always begin with 'U' or 'V'. Be careful!)

1. It's ..... use. He won't listen to reason.
2. ..... I understand it, this is the very best film on the market.
3. The young man walked ..... to the door and knocked, but nobody answered.
4. Until further ....., the company is not accepting any more applications for jobs.
5. "This is the very ..... house in which your grandfather lived when he was a boy."
6. "For various ..... I would rather not discuss this matter in public."
7. The very ..... of working all night makes me feel tired!
8. They say that the very ..... things in life are free!

9. Under these ..... we can't possibly meet the deadline.
10. My brother and his wife ..... us a visit at Christmas last year, but we haven't seen them since then.

"*Your time is up!*" We *urge* you to check your answers *as usual.* Have you gained *the upper hand?*

Key

I 1c, 2c, 3a, 4c, 5b, 6a, 7b
II 1b, 2b, 3a, 4c, 5c
III 1b, 2a, 3c, 4c
IV 1F, 2F, 3T, 4T 5T, 6T, 7T, 8T, 9F, 10F, 11F, 12F
V 1g, 2f, 3i, 4h, 5b, 6d, 7e, 8a, 9c
VI 1c, 2d, 3a, 4b
VII 1 umbrella, 2 voice, 3 voyage, 4 verses, 5 village, 6 valley, 7 view, 8 vegetables, 9 veils, 10 use, 11 virtue, 12 value
VIII 1 urge, 2 used, 3 use, 4 use, 5 visited, 6 voted, 7 unite, 8 used, used, 9 understand, 10 unloaded
IX 1 unhappy, 2 until, 3 vain, 4 understood, 5 under, 6 violent, 7 violent, 8 usual
X 1 no, 2 as, 3 up, 4 notice, 5 same, 6 reasons, 7 thought, 8 best, 9 circumstances, 10 paid

How many mistakes have you made?

	I to VI	VII to IX	X	
Excellent	0—4	0—3	1	mistakes
Good	5—8	4—6	2	mistakes
Satisfactory	9—12	7—9	3	mistakes
Not very good	13—20	10—15	4—5	mistakes
Weak	over 20	over 15	over 5	mistakes

WXY and Z

Was it worth while coming this far? *Wait and see! When* you finish this book, a new exciting *world welcomes* you.

I. What's the opposite?

1. A *man* always notices an attractive	a) woman. b) watch. c) wheel.
2. Do you prefer *winter* sports or	a) water sports? b) summer sports? c) snow sports?
3. Snow is *white;* coal is	a) yellow. b) black. c) red.
4. A *strong* person can easily influence a	a) weak person. b) wealthy person. c) wild person.
5. During every *war*, men have prayed for	a) despair. b) cruelty. c) peace.
6. Everything went *wrong* today; nothing went	a) false. b) right. c) hard.
7. Our swimming club *won* the first race, but	a) gained the second. b) started the second. c) lost the second.
8. Even if I *go to sleep* late, I still	a) while away the time. b) wake up early. c) wear out my clothes.
9. Do you usually wear your shoes *with* stockings or	a) without them? b) on top of them? c) next to them?
10. Our daughter doesn't feel *well;* she has been	a) fine since Thursday. b) ill since Thursday. c) cheerful since Thursday.

Don't worry about falling asleep. Study *works wonders!* It will keep you *wide awake!*

II. Which word or phrase has almost the same meaning?

1. *Something is in the wind.*
   a) It looks like snow.
   b) I smell smoke.
   c) Something's going to happen.

2. I *took him at his word.*
   a) believed him
   b) doubted him
   c) offended him

3. *What's wrong?*
   a) Where were you born?
   b) What's the matter?
   c) What's your name?

4. *In no way* did I mean to offend you.
   a) in cold blood
   b) in any case
   c) by no means

5. *He thinks the world of you.*
   a) You have disappointed him.
   b) He likes you very much.
   c) He blames you for everything.

6. Have you *had any word from* Robert since he joined the army?
   a) written to
   b) called on
   c) heard from

7. *On the whole* the winter has been quite mild.
   a) by and large
   b) all of a sudden
   c) for a short while

8. After the war, thousands of people were *out of work.*
   a) unemployed
   b) busy
   c) working out of doors.

9. "*Watch out for* that car!"
   a) start up
   b) don't worry about
   c) look out for

10. *Once in a while* I go out to dinner.
    a) sometimes
    b) gradually
    c) usually

11. After much confusion, the meeting finally *got under way.*
    a) ended
    b) began
    c) continued

III. Which choice makes sense?

1. Write it down
   a) before you forget it!
   b) before it flies away!
   c) before you remember it!

2. What a wonderful day!	a) Let's go for a walk! b) It's pouring! c) Quick, close the windows!
3. A good book is always	a) worthless. b) a waste of time. c) worth reading.
4. I wonder who he is.	a) I've never seen him before. b) I know him quite well. c) He is our neighbour.
5. Don't worry!	a) You can't keep your head above water. b) Things will turn out all right in the long run. c) Everything is going from bad to worse.
6. That can't wait until tomorrow!	a) You can take care of it next week. b) It can be done later. c) It must be done today.
7. I'm not ready to go yet.	a) Everything is in order. b) I can't find my keys. c) I have everything I need.
8. I had a terrible day at work.	a) It was worth while. b) Everything went wrong. c) I wish I could have stayed.
9. After the long walk we were so worn out that we	a) had to buy new clothes. b) went straight to bed. c) painted the kitchen.
10. There's no need to drive to the station.	a) It's a long way off. b) Something is in the wind. c) It's within walking distance.
11. The president's opinion carries a great deal of weight.	a) He has an important say in all political matters. b) No one ever listens to him. c) He really shouldn't eat so much.

IV. Is it true or false?

	T	F
1. Bears have wings.	☐	☐
2. Wheels are square.	☐	☐
3. Waiters repair cars.	☐	☐
4. Trees are made of wool.	☐	☐

	T	F
5. Dogs whistle.	☐	☐
6. Many French wines are world-famous.	☐	☐
7. A widow was once married.	☐	☐
8. Wonder and mystery often go together.	☐	☐
9. The wind blows.	☐	☐
10. Yesterday is past.	☐	☐
11. Roads have windows.	☐	☐
12. Children are young people.	☐	☐
13. There are twelve days in the week.	☐	☐
14. It's a waste to throw out useful things.	☐	☐
15. In cold weather you need warm clothes.	☐	☐

A short while ago you were a beginner. *The worst was yet to come.* Now, however, you can *put into words* most of your important thoughts.

V. Find the nouns which go together.

A. 1. waiter 2. watch 3. war 4. wave 5. window 6. wheat 7. wife

a) ocean, b) glass, c) time, d) husband, e) restaurant, f) battle, g) grain

B. 8. wages 9. weapon 10. wheel 11. wood 12. writer 13. wool 14. wing 15. wire

h) sheep, i) tree, j) work, k) electricity, l) gun, m) carriage, n) book, o) bird

VI. Find the words which go together.

1. to waste .....
2. to lose .....
3. to put .....
4. to go .....
5. to whistle .....

a) to work, b) into words, c) a tune, d) time, e) weight

VII. Put in the right noun.

1. When it's ripe, ... is harvested and made into flour.
2. There are four seasons in the .....—spring, summer, autumn and winter.
3. Many companies offer high ..... to experienced workers.
4. Even a deep ..... can run out of water.

5. One ..... at the trial described exactly what happened.
6. "Cold", "clear", "hot", "rainy" and "foggy" are words which describe the .....
7. You can express yourself in many different .....—such as singing, dancing, writing and painting.
8. The ..... consists of Saturday and Sunday.
9. A man with a strong ..... has great determination.
10. ..... are used to carry electricity and telephone messages.
11. You can't eat a lot of rich food and still expect to lose .....
12. ..... are used to fight with.
13. Poets use ..... in special ways.
14. A ..... is a married woman.
15. On the ..... home, we stopped for a drink.

Watch out for mistakes! You should still *write out* your answers so that you can check them. *You might as well* do things properly.

VIII. Put in the right verb.

1. Railway signals ..... drivers of approaching trains.
2. It's a good idea to ..... your hands before dinner.
3. Before we sent the parcel off, we had to ..... it in brown paper.
4. It's senseless to ..... money on things you don't need.
5. If you don't ..... your watch up, it'll stop.
6. I ..... I could stay longer, but I have to work tomorrow morning.
7. Long ago, singers and writers ..... from town to town throughout Europe.
8. If you have an accident, you may ..... your car or even lose your life.
9. Most machines ..... out after long hard use.
10. Farmers sometimes have to ..... animals such as horses and oxen in order to make them move.
11. If you ..... them every day, even your best shoes will soon wear out.
12. A strong man won't ..... to every desire.
13. When the river flooded, the bridge was ..... away.
14. After supper, I like to ..... the evening news on television.
15. Children can usually ..... at the age of two.
16. If you must speak to the person next to you during a concert, it's more polite to ..... than to talk in a loud voice.
17. I ..... to finish this book before I go to bed tonight.

IX. Put in the right adjective or adverb.

1. When it rains, everything gets .....
2. ..... people can afford expensive things.
3. The old bridge became so ..... that it was no longer safe to drive across it.
4. Which is ..... more to you—a new car or a trip abroad?
5. You're ..... to stay with us whenever you're in town.
6. Norway lies ..... of Sweden.
7. It was ..... to see my father again after so many years.
8. It's hard to tame a ..... animal!
9. The sea was so ..... that we could stay in it for hours without catching cold.
10. For a ..... person, old age is a long way off.
11. So many things—feelings, thoughts, memory, experience, hope, fear, desire—combine to make up a ..... person!

X. Put in the right word.

(It doesn't always begin with 'W,' 'X,' 'Y' or 'Z'. Be careful!)

1. "What ..... it rains tonight? We haven't got a tent!"
2. "I'm worn .....! Let's rest for a while."
3. In ancient Greece, Athens and Sparta were often ..... war with one another.
4. This morning I was wide ..... long before I had to get up.
5. The roof of the house ..... way under the weight of the snow.
6. "What ..... me? I want to go too!"
7. "It's so late that you ..... as well spend the night here. We have plenty of room."
8. My brother once had a serious road accident. That's ..... he drives so carefully now.
9. We watched television ..... a while and then went to bed.
10. The mechanic took the young boy ..... his wing and taught him everything he knew about cars.
11. Business agreements are usually ..... writing.
12. The doctor ..... me waiting for half an hour while he spoke to another patient.
13. "I don't know what's inside the parcel. Wait and .....!"
14. The course was difficult, but Paul stuck to it and managed to keep his ..... above water.
15. We could hear thunder in the distance, but the storm was still a ..... way off.
16. Most of the city's beautiful houses were pulled down in order to ..... way for the modern streets and buildings which you see today.

17. "I've looked ..... and wide for a copy of that book!"
18. "I would ..... go shopping tomorrow than today, if that's all right with you."
19. Modern medicine can ..... wonders!
20. I can't quite ..... into words the feeling I had when I saw him.
21. "Don't .....! I'll take care of everything!"
22. "Well, I must go ..... work now. I'll see you this evening."
23. "..... yet we have received no news of the missing boys."
24. This winter the weather was quite mild. The temperature seldom dropped ..... zero.
25. "Shall I warm ..... some soup for lunch?"
26. A great deal of fresh food ..... to waste when workers at the nation's ports went on strike and refused to unload ships.
27. "You're right ..... a way, but I can understand Mike's point of view too."
28. "Have it your ..... way, but if anything goes wrong you'll be held responsible!"
29. "Please write the instructions ..... in full for me, just in case I need to refer to them later."
30. "..... the way, did you ever receive a letter from Linda?"
31. "Things are going from ..... to worse. Two weeks ago I lost my job, and now my wife is ill."
32. "..... other words, as I understand it, you don't believe him."

We wish we could stay, but it's the end! So we'll *wish* you good luck and leave you *with* the last answers. And *what about you? Well*, now you're on your own!

Key

I 1a, 2b, 3b, 4a, 5c, 6b, 7c, 8b, 9a, 10b
II 1c, 2a, 3b, 4c, 5b, 6c, 7a, 8a, 9c, 10a, 11b
III 1a, 2a, 3c, 4a, 5b, 6c, 7b, 8b, 9b, 10c, 11a
IV 1F, 2F, 3F, 4F, 5F, 6T, 7T, 8T, 9T, 10T, 11F, 12T, 13F, 14T, 15T
V A. 1e, 2c, 3f, 4a, 5b, 6g, 7d — B. 8j, 9l, 10m, 11i, 12n, 13h, 14o, 15k
VI 1d, 2e, 3b, 4a, 5c
VII 1 wheat, 2 year, 3 wages, 4 well, 5 witness, 6 weather, 7 ways, 8 week-end, 9 will, 10 wires, 11 weight, 12 weapons, 13 words, 14 wife, 15 way
VIII 1 warn, 2 wash, 3 wrap, 4 waste, 5 wind, 6 wish, 7 wandered, 8 wreck, 9 wear, 10 whip, 11 wear, 12 yield, 13 washed, 14 watch, 15 walk, 16 whisper, 17 want
IX 1 wet, 2 wealthy, 3 weak, 4 worth, 5 welcome, 6 west, 7 wonderful, 8 wild, 9 warm, 10 young, 11 whole

X 1 if, 2 out, 3 at, 4 awake, 5 gave, 6 about, 7 might, 8 why, 9 for, 10 under, 11 in, 12 kept, 13 see, 14 head, 15 long, 16 make, 17 far, 18 rather, 19 work, 20 put, 21 worry, 22 to, 23 as, 24 below, 25 up, 26 went, 27 in, 28 own, 29 out, 30 by, 31 bad, 32 in

How many mistakes have you made?

	I to VI	VII to IX	X	
Excellent	0— 7	0— 4	0— 3	mistakes
Good	8—14	5— 8	4— 6	mistakes
Satisfactory	15—21	9—12	7—10	mistakes
Not very good	22—34	13—22	11—16	mistakes
Weak	over 34	over 22	over 16	mistakes

Taking Stock

At last you have reached the end. All that remains to be done now is to check your results. Are you satisfied with them?

Letter A	I—VI	VII—IX	X .....
Letter B	I—VI	VII—IX	X .....
Letter C	I—VI	VII—IX	X .....
Letter D	I—VI	VII—IX	X .....
Letter E	I—VI	VII—IX	X .....
Letter F	I—VI	VII—IX	X .....
Letter G	I—VI	VII—IX	X .....
Letter H	I—VI	VII—IX	X .....
Letters IJK	I—VI	VII—IX	X .....
Letter L	I—VI	VII—IX	X .....
Letter M	I—VI	VII—IX	X .....
Letter N	I—VI	VII—IX	X .....
Letter O	I—VI	VII—IX	X .....
Letters PQ	I—VI	VII—IX	X .....
Letter R	I—VI	VII—IX	X .....
Letter S	I—VI	VII—IX	X .....
Letter T	I—VI	VII—IX	X .....
Letters UV	I—VI	VII—IX	X .....
Letters WXYZ	I—VI	VII—IX	X .....

Now read page 95 through again. The advice on that page still applies.